*Library
Media
Projects
for the Gifted*

Library
Media
Projects
for the Gifted

M. Ellen Jay

Bunny,
Knowing you are always
there to share things
with is important
to me.
Ellen

LIBRARY PROFESSIONAL PUBLICATIONS
1982

First published 1982 as a Library Professional Publication,
an imprint of The Shoe String Press, Inc.,
Hamden, Connecticut 06514

Printed in the United States of America

   .

Library of Congress Cataloging in Publication Data

Jay, M. Ellen.
  Library media projects for the gifted
  Bibliography: p.
  Includes index.
  1. Libraries and students. 2. Gifted children—
Education. 3. School libraries. I. Title.
Z718.7.J38 1982   025.5′6′088375   82-4665
ISBN 0-208-01940-5
ISBN 0-208-01922-7 (pbk.)

Contents

Introduction

According to recent reports, gifted children—about two million of them—constitute from 3% to 5% of the school population. These include those who have creative talents in a variety of fields, those whose academic ability is high and those whose performance is outstanding. They come from all walks of life, all economic and social strata, and all geographic areas. Yet, fewer than 4% of these children are being provided with the opportunities they need to develop their unique capabilities—and this at a time when the future calls out for leadership and brilliant performance.

Librarians who serve children through both public and school library media programs are in a unique position to help them uncover their own special abilities and gifts. School library personnel in particular, who work with the same children in a special teaching relationship week after week, are in an extraordinarily good position to observe the many facets of a personality, and to discover it informed by a sense of humor, curiosity, originality, imagination, verbal ability, quick perceptions, and passionate interests. The librarian may make a great contribution as catalyst for discovery of children whose gifts, because of deprivation or handicap—physical, emotional, cultural or social—may otherwise never emerge.

Gifted children need time, an open and stimulating environment, and patient adult listeners and sounding boards. They flourish with exposure to those adults who enjoy deciding among alternatives, who understand the gifted child's need to analyze and synthesize, and who recognize the pleasure that comes from solving problems and relating previously unconnected ideas. The assumption is frequently made that because gifted students are avid readers, possess good vocabularies, and have a broad factual knowledge base they are also efficient library media center users. This is not always the case. While they may in fact relish finding and using information, gifted students may not have the skill needed to search and sort materials, to locate information within these materials, and to produce a research project. Development of such skills requires guidance and instruction, and must be learned through practice. Such search skills are an important component of learning for all students, but they are essential tools for gifted and talented students who are to take full advantage of their intellectual abilities.

The bulk of this book consists of sample activities designed for use by a cooperating team of classroom and library media teachers. Each activity includes descriptions of the necessary materials, the procedures, the student product, and a time commitment for development and completion. These activities will serve to introduce concepts, provide practice, and allow time for realistic applications. Activities will be grouped according to their relationship to 1) search skills, 2) report writing, 3) open-ended activity, and 4) curriculum-related activity. Multiple activities related to a specific skill are sequenced according to difficulty.

For gifted children more than any others, the two are inseparable: enjoy and learn!

Part I
Involvement of Library Media Personnel
in Instructional Programs for the Gifted Student

The need to provide appropriate academic challenges for gifted and talented students appears to have substantial support among educators, although there is still some fear that the charge of elitism will be leveled at programs that identify some students as being more able than others. At the present time, all but five state departments of education have at least a portion of one person's time allocated to directing and coordinating gifted and talented programs; all but nine states have budgets for gifted and talented programs. Furthermore, a total of 149 colleges and universities offer graduate programs in gifted and talented education. The literature provides solid research-based evidence of the need for such programs, and perhaps indeed they are gaining in acceptance by the public because of greater emphasis and an increasing number of children being identified who could benefit by them. In recent years more schools have become aware that the potential for giftedness is not limited to children of middle or upper class status and have begun to look for gifted children among poor and minority-group children as well.

Characteristics of Giftedness

Initial attempts to identify gifted students relied upon a single measure: the I.Q. score. Through research and practical experience a more complex concept of giftedness has emerged. This has necessitated the use of multiple screening measures in an attempt to identify gifted students within various given populations. While specific terms may differ, there appears to be general agreement as to the characteristics of gifted students:

1. Their interests at a very early age extend beyond the self. They are likely, even in elementary school, to display keen concern with morality, problems of international relations

and world peace. Their curiosity is avid. They read more than average children, have much longer attention spans, and apply themselves with enthusiasm to self-directed projects. (E.L. Horowitz, "Educating the Gifted Child," *Gifted Child Quarterly*, vol. 18, pp. 17–21.)

2. An academically gifted child will learn more quickly and will probe more deeply into the topic than will his/her average classmate. An academically gifted child will display greater independence and self-initiative than will his/her average ability classmates. The academically gifted child will read more and display a greater interest in reading than will average ability classmates. (J.D. Mulhern, "The Gifted Child in the Regular Classroom," *Roeper Review*, vol. 1, no. 1, 1978, p. 4.)

3. Identifying characteristics include: Good memory, good vocabulary, learns quickly and easily a large fund of information, can abstract and generalize, produces many ideas, is flexible and original, sees new ways and unusual ways to do things, elaborates by adding details, is intense and concentrates, creates products, shares a high level of enthusiasm, is involved, and shows perseverance. (P.T. Colon and D.J. Treffinger, "Providing for the Gifted in the Regular Classroom—Am I Really MAD?" *Roeper Review*, vol. 3, no. 2, 1980, p. 19.)

4. Renzulli and Hartman group characteristics into four main types: 1) Learning—unusually advanced vocabulary, richness of expression and elaboration; possesses a storehouse of information about a variety of topics; wants to know what makes things "tick"; usually "sees more" or "gets more" out of a story, film, etc. than others; visually literate; reads a great deal independently, prefers adult books; 2) Motivation—becomes absorbed and truly involved in certain topics; is easily bored with routine tasks; is self-critical and a perfectionist; prefers to work independently; is concerned with adult problems; is assertive or even stubborn in beliefs; 3) Creativity—displays a great deal of curiosity about anything and everything; often offers unusual, unique, or clever responses; sees humor in situations that may not be humorous to others; aware of impulses and more sensitive to them; is sensitive to beauty; 4) Leadership—carries responsibility well and can be counted on; seems to be well liked by class-

mates; generally directs the activity in which he/she is involved; is flexible in thought and action; excels in athletic activities and is well coordinated. (Cited by M. Bireley, in *Ohio Media Spectrum*, Summer 1978, pp. 15-17.)

These characteristics of giftedness—advanced reading interests, self-motivation, curiosity, originality, and the ability to learn quickly and in depth—help identify the needs which should be addressed by programs designed for gifted and talented students and, at the same time, indicate the kinds of programs that will meet their needs.

Torrence suggests that gifted students need freedom to wonder, to experiment, to risk, to find out what is possible, to discover their limits and to decide what fits. (E.P. Torrence, "The Gifted Child's Major Problem," in *Gifted Child Quarterly*, vol. 15, pp. 147-155.) Isaacs identifies the need for a reading program that meets the needs of the child who is reading when he or she enters kindergarten or first grade. (A.F. Isaacs, "Keeping Giftedness Turned on May Be Elementary," in *Gifted Child Quarterly*, vol. 16, pp. 143-145.) Renzulli suggests that young children can, in fact, be designers and creators of many unique things, but first we must teach them to think like real inquirers rather than lesson learners, and then we must provide the methodological resources and types of learning environments that will help them transcend the usual student role of being a mere doer of exercises. (J. Renzulli, Mimeographed paper cited by J. Wiles and J. Bondi in "Teaching for Creative Thinking in the Intermediate Grades," in *Roeper Review*, vol. 3, no. 1, 1980, p. 5.)

Meeting the Needs of the Gifted

A number of approaches are used to attempt to meet the needs of gifted and talented students. *Pullout programs* identify certain youngsters and then "pull them out" of regular classroom activity for a period of time during which special programs are provided for them. *Acceleration programs* move identified children ahead to allow them to work on material that they are ready for regardless of chronological age. *Enrichment programs* are designed to provide additional activities within the regular classroom for children identified as gifted. These additional activities can vary from merely assigning more work of the same type, to providing creative, open-ended assignments to be completed along with regular classroom assignments. While a small number of gifted students are placed in special classes, or attend special schools, the majority of them spend a considerable amount of time in regular classroom situations. This presents classroom teachers with the problem of providing sufficient repetition and practice for the majority of class members without becoming overly redundant (and boring) for the gifted youngsters.

There has been a good deal of research done which has improved our capability in identifying gifted and talented students, but which is primarily designed to be useful in organized programs and not in individual classrooms. Since large numbers of gifted youngsters spend the majority of their time in regular classroom settings, their classroom teachers need a means of providing the essential augmented experiences while retaining primary responsibility for the student's basic learning program. This means a process of coordination for the teacher, of monitoring independent student projects which sharpen interest in mainstream classroom instruction. This enables the gifted youngster to remain very much a part of his classroom peer group and contribute his share to classroom learning while going beyond it.

A good solution to this challenge has proved to be the intensified utilization of the school library media center and the services of its trained library media teachers and support staff. In many instances, an informal bond develops between gifted students and library media specialists because of the materials the library has available, and because of the natural empathy young people feel for adults who take time and interest in listening to their ideas. The gifted and talented student will often just gravitate to the library media center, and make it his own learning and support center, because that is where the books and other materials are that help him to satisfy his many interests. The center provides a work environment in keeping with the need for self-directed inquiry; the library media specialists have the training to help the students develop search skills and locate needed materials.

The environment of the library media center is less restrictive than that of most classrooms. The student is able to pursue a topic in greater depth than is generally possible within the regular curriculum, and may do so through independent study, with assistance as required. Within the library media center program the student has access to many different options of format: print and nonprint sources, reference and recreational material, commercially produced materials, and supplies and equipment used to produce materials of his own. School library media centers are rapidly becoming equipped with micro-computers and other technologies that enable students to learn to manipulate information in many formats. There is a time flexibility in the library media center that is not possible within the class period structure. The student need not stop working because it is time for groups to change activities. Arrangements can be made for the gifted student to continue on a given project as long as desired under the supervision of the library media teacher. In short, the library media program is prepared to supply the very kinds of opportunities associated with instruction of the gifted.

Today's library media teachers are indeed trained as teachers, as well as specialists in acquiring, organizing and utilizing information resources. Their expertise is not limited to the materials actually housed within the walls of a school's library media center because, through the resource sharing networks in which they are now involved, they can tap into many wider resources locally, even at the state and national level. Highly specialized collections of materials— journals, printouts, maps and documents, among others—can be searched and consulted by gifted students, available through their own school library media center from industry, universities, state and national archives.

Today's library media teachers can bring rich human resources into the orbit of their gifted and talented students: scientists, artists, policy makers for government, and many others. They can find and bring students together with specialists from every community's increasingly rich resource of retired people who are eager to inflame the imaginations of gifted and talented students with their own enthusiasms and experiences.

Today's library media teachers are prepared to work with individuals or with small groups of students in a discovery approach to learning. Problem-solving skills they have learned in the process of locating information can be shared with students, as well as more traditional instruction in the techniques of finding and using materials fully and efficiently.

In addition, today's library media teachers are able to provide visibility and a forum for the products of learning. Projects such as slide tape programs, video tapes, models, charts, research papers, and innovative computer games can be cataloged and lent to others through the library media center. If standards of accuracy and technical quality are maintained in the process of production, student-produced materials can be useful resources for others.

While it is true that not all library media center programs at present can provide the kind of environment described, many do, and the potential for such an environment is there. The collection can be expanded, the staff can work to develop skills related to meeting the needs of the gifted and talented, and students can benefit to the extent that the school's administration expects such a goal, and vigorously supports its achievement.

Requirement: Teamwork

In order for an affirmative and planned program for gifted and talented students to be available to those who need it, there must be active, on-going collaboration between the library media and classroom varieties of teacher. Responsibilities for activities must be divided, understood and met by both parties. There must be joint planning time which allows for carefully allocating these responsibilities and structuring their implementation. In general, the classroom teacher retains the responsibility for determining due dates, work schedules, and the grading of student products. The library media teacher researches the specifics of the assignment, develops resource choices, and provides related instruction.

Success of any joint venture requires enthusiasm and the determination that it will succeed by all concerned in it. In some instances, the administration may find it necessary to provide for development through in-service sessions of staff understanding of the team approach and how collaboration can improve learning opportunities for gifted and talented children.

Administrative support fosters teamwork, but it also requires an attitude on the part of faculty members which places the highest priority on developing student potentials rather than on protecting their own "free" time. The reality of the occasional uncommitted teacher—classroom or library media—and that of personality conflicts which can hinder the development of the desired collaboration must be faced and somehow overcome. One way to eliminate most such problems is for administrators not only to evidence a strong commitment and assign a high priority to cooperative activities, but to insure that this priority is reflected in evaluation procedures.

Requirement: Administrative Commitment and Support

The degree of support a program receives from the building

level administrator has the most major impact upon its success or failure. With the full support of the principal, a library media center program can provide handsomely for the needs of the gifted and talented students as well as serve the other students.

The scheduling of the library media teacher's time is one important particular which reflects the degree of the administrator's commitment. If scheduling is done primarily with a view to providing breaks for the classroom teachers, then mounting the type of program for the gifted and talented that we have been proposing becomes next to impossible. If, on the other hand, a more flexible open schedule is mandated, then the needs of all the children can be met. Classes can then be permitted to schedule time in the library media center as needed rather than operate on rigid terms whereby because it is 10:00 A.M. on Tuesday, a given class stops what it is doing in the classroom and marches to the library media center. Rigid use projects library media center time as an interlude unrelated to real learning, or as an unproductive interruption. Open scheduling allows for individuals or small groups to work in and out of the library media center, harnessing its resources and services to what they are doing and what they could be doing with any given unit of work. Students should never be limited to signing a book out only at a scheduled time, or only using the center for reference on a weekly prescribed day. When whole classes do go, as they should, to the library media center it is with a sense of purpose and awareness that meaningful instruction can take place. The media specialist's time can be balanced among individual, small group, and total class instruction. Such a scheduling format can be implemented only with the enthusiastic support of the building level administrator.

A further indication of administrative support is related to the establishment of a total, unified collection. If all instructional materials within the building are processed through the media center, cataloged, and distributed through a central location, then everyone has access to all materials. In contrast, when materials are purchased by and housed in individual classrooms, with no centralized control system, their accessibility is limited. Centralized cataloging does *not* mean that materials may not be purchased at the request of an individual teacher or grade, nor does this plan preclude signing out materials to individuals or grades for long periods of time. However, when the availability of materials is known to all, appropriate arrangements can be made for their use as needed. With the implementation of centralized cataloging, materials are less likely to be overlooked when they would be the most useful and beneficial.

Library media teachers charged with the responsibility of selecting materials to support a gifted program need to expand the criteria generally used to evaluate materials for purchase. In addition to considerations of accuracy, technical quality, and relationship to curriculum, some materials selected must be flexible, open-ended and versatile. They need to stimulate divergent thinking, originality and creativity, rather than just providing facts to be memorized. When appropriate, materials should be issue-oriented and usable in a number of learning situations. Materials should challenge students to employ higher levels of thinking such as analysis, synthesis, and evaluation. Information should be presented with the aim of being *applied* in some manner rather than merely recalled at will. Materials should provide students with opportunities to draw conclusions, to generalize, and to suggest other applications.

In developing a collection designed to support a gifted and talented program, special attention should be given to the reference collection. Specialized reference materials are needed in addition to the usual encyclopedias, atlases, and almanacs. Included also should be specialized biographical, geographical, scientific, and literary references; this is equally true whether the collection is for elementary, middle, or secondary school levels. The quantity and sophistication of the individual items selected will vary, but the need for representative works exists at all levels. If gifted and talented elementary students (or any other students for that matter) are limited to general encyclopedias as a reference source, they will continue to limit themselves out of habit. If, on the other hand, they are exposed to the notion that specialized references exist for every topic and provide essential information, they will expand their search patterns. Suggestions for a basic reference collection appear in Appendix 2.

Part II
Sample Activities

While the activities included here can be adapted to develop skills desirable in all students, they are most suited for use with gifted students. The nature of the activities matches the characteristics of the gifted student.

The search skill activities, such as use of indexes and specialized references books, are introduced to gifted students at an earlier age than they are to students of average ability. This is to foster their ability to work independently and to pursue topics of their own interests.

Open-ended activities provide outlets for the gifted students' creativity, originality, divergent thinking, and willingness to pursue a topic to a greater depth. Activities concerned with idioms, humor, puns, and symbolism are of interest to them because of their increased verbal abilities.

Curriculum-related activities provide an opportunity to enlarge and broaden the students' experiences. While related to classroom units of study, they allow students to pursue topics of individual interest keeping them interested and challenged.

In keeping with the overall objective of providing students with the skills necessary to become efficient, independent users of instructional materials, use of search skills should be presented and mastered as a basis for developing other skills.

Index Activities

Since indexes provide the most efficient means of locating complete information on a subject, skills related to use of indexes should be dealt with first. Students need to be able to interpret abbreviations, format clues, and idiosyncracies such as word-by-word or letter-by-letter alphabetizing systems.

#1   Introduction to indexes

Concepts
1. An index helps one to locate specific information quickly.
2. An index is arranged in alphabetical order.
3. An index is usually found at the end of a book or in the last volume of a multi-volume set.
4. Items which are indented are a part of the topic which preceded the indention. These visual clues are important.

Materials
A set of text books of sufficient number to allow each student to have an identical copy.

A set of questions developed by the teacher derived from the topics listed in the index of the text being used for the lesson. (It is important that all students have the same edition of the text being used so as to have identical indexes and page number references.)

Procedures
1. Introduce concepts 1 through 4 during a discussion.
2. Follow up with questions requesting students to cite the page number where specific information is found. (As students' skill increases, the teacher should increase the difficulty of the questions. For example, ask on what page a map, a chart or a picture of something might be found. If the topic covers more than one page, students will have to scan the pages to locate the answer to the question.)
3. Request some topics which involve *see* and *see also* references.

Student Products
Verbal answers (Make sure each student participates.)

Time Commitment
A single class session.

Adaptations
Have students suggest questions for the group.

#2 Scavenger hunt

Concepts
1. An index helps one locate specific information quickly.
2. An index is arranged alphabetically.
3. Items which are indented are a part of the topic which precedes the indention. These visual clues are important.

Materials
A set of textbooks of sufficient number to allow each student to have an identical copy.

Procedures
1. Divide students into two teams.
2. Have each team develop a set of questions based upon the index of the text being used.
3. Questions should be written down, and the page number where the information is located should be cited.
4. Questions should be turned in to the teacher.
5. The teacher should make sure that the two sets of questions used for the contest are of comparable difficulty.
6. At a later date the scavenger hunt is held. This is done by providing each team the questions developed by the other team.
7. The winner is the team which locates the answers in the shortest amount of time.

Student Products
A set of questions (with answers cited) developed by team.
A team answer sheet filled in at the time of the competition.

Time Commitment
Two class sessions one week apart; the first to develop the questions and the second to answer them.

Adaptations
As skills improve, a variety of books could be used rather than a text set.

Sample Questions
1. On what page will you find a diagram of the water cycle? (p. 27)
2. On what page will you find a definition of a jungle? (p. 54)
3. On what page will you find a picture of Robert E. Lee? (p. 146)
4. What would you have to look under to find information about oil? (Under petroleum.) (p. 243)

5. How many pages are there devoted to gold? (Count pages under subtopics such as jewelry, mining, etc.)

Sample Answer Sheet

Question #_____ Found on Page_____

#3   Find the fact

Concepts
1. An index helps one locate specific information quickly.
2. An index is arranged alphabetically.
3. Items which are indented are a part of the topic which precedes the indention. These visual clues are important.

Materials
A reserve collection of 20 to 30 nonfiction titles selected from the library media center collection. All must contain indexes.
A variety of subject areas should be included among books.
A supply of index cards.

Procedures
1. The teacher generates a question based upon the index of each title included in the reserve collection.
2. Select a fact that is not likely to be ready background knowledge. Choose something of interest but which is off the beaten track.
3. Be certain that the information can be located within the book by use of the index, and requires no more than a paragraph to a page of reading to locate the needed information.
4. Type each question on a 3x5 card. Include on the card the title and call number of the book to be used in answering the question.
5. Number the cards.
6. Locate question cards so that they are available to students.

Student Products
A sheet of paper for writing down the answers to the questions.
Paper numbered to match the number of question cards. Beside each number, write the fact which answers the question and the page where the answer was found. Questions may be answered in any sequence.

Time Commitment
About a week should be sufficient time for students to answer all questions.

Adaptations
Question cards can be posted on a display board, filed in a box, or placed in the pocket of the book used for the question. Putting the cards on a display board helps insure that they will remain for the duration of the activity. However, either of the other methods allows

the students to take the cards with them while working on the answers. There are advantages and disadvantages to both systems. This type of activity can be done with a class group if each student begins with a different question so as to avoid undue congestion and demand for the same book.

This can also serve as a learning center activity to be completed during independent study time by individual students.

Sample Questions

1. Where does a silverfish live?
   574 *Naming Living Things* by Reedman p. 68

2. What does the term "suitcase farmer" mean?
   330.978 *Dust Bowl* by Lauber p. 49

3. What was Hank O'Day's job?
   796.357 *More Strange But True Baseball Stories* p. 50, 52, 54

4. What was a crucible used for?
   621.909 *Tools In Your Life* by Adler p. 58

These questions are meant to serve as examples. Actual questions used with a group of students must be created based upon materials in the collection to be used.

#4 *Interpreting abbreviations used in indexes of multi-volume works*

Concepts
1. The index is usually found in the last volume. (In some cases there is an index in the back of each volume.)
2. Abbreviations are used to indicate a specific volume where information is located.
3. Sequence of numbers and letters, kind of type face, and the actual symbols all have specific significance and must be interpreted properly if the desired information is to be found.
4. While the specific symbols vary from index to index, every index uses a systematic set of abbreviations.
5. These special symbols are usually explained at the beginning of the index.
6. More information will be found by using the index than by going directly to the volume the user thinks will contain the needed information.

Materials
A selection of general encyclopedias with index volumes included.
A list of topics which according to the index are included in several of the volumes.
An answer sheet form for each student. (See sample)

Procedures
1. Produce the students' answer sheet using the questions given in the example. Questions will be identical for each topic.
2. Develop a list of topics suitable for the questions.
3. Each student is assigned one topic.
4. Students will answer the questions by looking up their topics in each of the general encyclopedias provided.

Student Products
Completed answer sheet.

Time Commitment
One class period to introduce the concepts and to assign topics and distribute answer sheets.
One week for individual work to complete the answer sheets.

Adaptations
Have students identify which encyclopedia is their "favorite" and give reasons for the choice.

Sample Answer Sheet

Name _____

Assigned topic _____ (Butterfly) _____

1. How many pages of information would you find if you went directly to the volume without using the index?

Encyclopedia #1 _____ (title) _____   Pages _____ (6 pages) _____

Encyclopedia #2 _____   _____

Encyclopedia #3 _____   _____

2. How many pages of information would you find it you followed the leads in the index?

Encyclopedia #1 _____   _____

Encyclopedia #2 _____   _____

Encyclopedia #3 _____   _____

3. How many different volumes contain information related to your topic?

Encyclopedia #1 _____   Volumes _____

Encyclopedia #2 _____   _____

Encyclopedia #3 _____   _____

4. Which encyclopedia provides you with the most information about your topic?

Title _____ Pages _____ Entries _____

and Special features _____

#5 Two ways to alphabetize

Concepts
1. There are two ways to alphabetize index entries.
2. Entries will be in different places depending upon which system of alphabetizing is being used.
3. Letter-by-letter system considers each letter as it comes and ignores ends of words.
4. Word-by-word system is based upon the idea that nothing comes before something and stops at the end of each word.
5. Letter-by-letter system is used WITHIN the word even when words are arranged using the word-by-word system.

Examples:

Letter-by-letter system	Word-by-word system
NEWARK	NEW BRITAIN
NEW BRITAIN	NEW YORK
NEW YORK	NEW ZEALAND
NEW ZEALAND	NEWARK

Materials
A worksheet with examples to be arranged in order using both systems of alphabetizing.

Procedures
1. Teacher presents the class with a list of entries and asks students to put these into alphabetical order. Students will probably apply the rules for letter-by-letter alphabetizing because of previous experience.
2. Teacher lists the entries using word-by-word system.
3. Discussion follows as to the existence of two systems of alphabetizing, the rules for each, and where one would encounter each system of alphabetizing.
4. Teacher gives directions for completing the worksheets.

Student Products
A worksheet with lists of entries arranged correctly by both letter-by-letter and word-by-word systems of alphabetizing.

Time Commitment
One class period or possibly overnight to complete the worksheet.

Adaptations
Have students develop a list of entries (five or so) which would be sequenced differently using the two systems of alphabetizing.

Sample (with answers filled in)

Name _____

Arrange Each Set of Words Alphabetically.

First, number the blanks on the left using letter-by-letter alphabetizing. Next, number the blanks on the right using word-by-word alphabetizing. In each case, place a 1 before the word which comes first, a 2 in front of the word that would come next, etc.

Letter		Word	Letter		Word
6	New Zealand	3	6	Air pressure	3
3	Newman	5	1	Airborne	4
1	New Britain	1	4	Airplane	5
5	Newtown	6	2	Air Force	1
4	New Rochelle	2	3	Air mattress	2
2	Newcombe	4	5	Airport	6

Letter		Word	Letter		Word
6	Isolation	6	1	Old	1
5	Is land there	3	6	Old timer	4
3	Islam	4	4	Old Man River	3
2	Is Anybody Out There	2	2	Olden	5
4	Island	5	3	Old Glory	2
1	Is	1	5	Oldster	6

#6 *Application of the two ways to alphabetize*

Concepts
1. There are two systems of alphabetizing.
2. As a searcher, one must use the same system to locate information that the editor used to create the index.

Materials
Selected reference books which employ both systems of alphabetizing in their respective indexes.
A list of topics to be looked up in these reference books.

Procedures
1. Identify reference books within the collection which employ each system of alphabetizing entries.
2. Create a list of topics to be looked up which require the searcher to apply the correct alphabetizing system in order to locate the entry.
3. Present students with the list of topics and the books. Have students look up the topics and on their paper give the topic, the book found in, the page it would be on according to the index, and the system of alphabetizing used in that book.

Student Products
Answer sheet giving the information requested for each topic on the list.

Time Commitment
One class period to present the assignment and begin work, and a week of independent work to finish the assignment.

Adaptations
Have students determine the system of alphabetizing used in selected reference books by just looking through the indexes. Have students support their opinions with sequences of entries they find in the indexes which prove their conclusions.

Sample Answer Sheet

Name _____

Find Each of the Terms Listed in the Index of a Reference Book and Give the Information Requested for Each:

	term	where found	page	alphabetic system
1.	Lakewood, Ohio	Rand McNally World Atlas	248	Letter
2.	Treaty of Newport	Langer's Encyclopedia of World History	1241	Word
3.	To Kill a Mockingbird	_____	_____	_____
4.	Old Man And the Sea	_____	_____	_____

Note: This example is intended to provide the format for an answer sheet. A complete set of terms is not given because the terms used by an individual must be selected from materials in the collection to be used by the students. When selecting terms for use remember to select terms that would be in different locations in the index depending on the system of alphabetizing being used.

Examples of indexes which employ
letter-by-letter alphabetizing: Most general encyclopedias; most specialized dictionaries, such as:
Brewer's Dictionary of Phrase And Fable, Webster's New Geographical Dictionary, and Reader's Encyclopedia

Examples of indexes which employ word-by-word alphabetizing: The card catalog; Americana Encyclopedia; Oxford Companion series
to American Literature, to English Literature, Music, etc.; Encyclopedia of World History by Langer.

#7   *Using indexes to create a bibliography*

Concepts

All concepts introduced and practiced in the preceding index activities. (If students do not already know how to write bibliographies, use Activity on Bibliographic Forms p. 66)

Materials

Reference section and card catalog in the library media center.

Procedures

1. Each student is given a topic.
2. They are to locate all available information on their given topic by using the various indexes available in the media center.

Student Products

Each student will produce a bibliography on the topic assigned. The bibliography will be the result of searching all the indexes available, i.e., general encyclopedias, specialized reference materials, card catalog, and individual trade books. It should be as complete as possible.

Time Commitment

Two weeks of independent work should be given initially and extended if appropriate. The nature of the topics selected will in part determine the time needed to complete the assignment. Broader topics will require more time than specific topics. Topics selected need to be broad enough to allow for some divergent thinking in terms of related information, but should not be so broad as to become limitless.

Adaptations

Several students could be given the same topic introducing an element of competition in terms of who produced the most complete bibliography.

Table of Contents Activity
Find the fact

Concepts

1. Table of contents helps locate specific information.
2. Table of contents is arranged in the order in which information appears in the book.
3. Items which are indented are a part of the topic which precedes the indention.

Materials

A reserve collection of twenty to thirty nonfiction titles selected from the library media center collection which contain tables of contents. A variety of subject areas should be included among the books.
A supply of index cards.

Procedures

1. Teacher generates a question based upon the table of contents of each title included in the reserve collection.
2. Select a fact that is not likely to be ready background knowledge. Choose something of interest but which is off the beaten track. Be certain that the information can be located within the book by use of the table of contents and requires no more than a paragraph to a page of reading to locate.
3. Type each question on a 3x5 card.
4. Include on the card the title and call number of the book to be used in answering the question.
5. Number the cards sequentially.
6. Locate cards conveniently for students.

Student Products

A sheet of paper numbered to match the questions, with answers to each question and the page number where the answer was found. (Questions may be answered in any sequence.)

Time Commitment

About a week should be sufficient time for students to answer all the questions.

Adaptations

Question cards can be posted on a display board, filed in a box, or placed in the pocket of the book used for the activity. Putting the cards on a display board helps insure that they will remain for the duration of the activity. However, either of the other methods allows the students to take the cards with them while working on the answers. There are advantages and disadvantages to both systems. This type of activity can be done with a class group if each student begins with a different question so as to avoid undue congestion and demand for the same book.

This can also serve as a learning center activity to be completed during independent study time by individual students.

Sample Questions

1. Name two types of engines of the future.

    621.4 *Engines* by Meyer use chapter titled "Engines of the future" pp. 71-74

2. What measurement term was used to mean the length of the forearm from the elbow to the tip of the middle finger?

    389 *Things That Measure* by Carona use chapter titled "The use of arms for measurement" p. 13

3. What jobs are given to reindeer by Laplanders?

    636 *Animals That Help Us* by Fenton use chapter titled "Reindeer" p. 105

4. Name a plant that will grow best in a sunny and dry terrarium.

    574.074 *Terrariums* by Hoke use chapter titled "Plants: which kinds" subhead "sunny and dry" p. 26

These questions are meant to serve as examples. Actual questions used with a group of students must be created based upon materials in the collection to be used.

General Encyclopedia Activities

Because the general encyclopedia articles provide a good first stop for acquiring information about a topic, skill in using them should be introduced in the primary grades. Attention given to the use of indexes, subheadings and special features of these encyclopedias expands their usefulness.

#1 Introduction to encyclopedias: Finding an entry

Concepts
1. Entries are arranged alphabetically.
2. Outside of volume indicates what letter(s) are inside.

Materials
Set of encyclopedias.
Worksheet.

Procedures
1. Select topics for which multi-paged articles are included.
2. Choose articles in which an illustration appears on the first page of article.
3. Make up a worksheet which asks students to locate the start of an article and something about the picture that is on the first page of the article. (The sample worksheet is based on *World Book Encyclopedia*.)
4. Present the concepts to the students.
5. Hand out the worksheets.
6. Provide help as needed.

Student Products
Completed worksheets.

Time Commitment
Probably a week would be adequate.

Adaptations
Look up the same topic in another general encyclopedia.

Encyclopedia Worksheet #1

1. Look up Animal. What page does it start on?___
   Name one animal you see on that page _____

2. Look up Food. What page does it start on?_____
   Name three kinds of food you see in the picture:

   _____   _____   _____

3. Look up Dog. What page does it start on?_____
   What do you see in the picture on that page?

   _____

4. Look up Heat. What page does it start on? _____
   List four sources of heat: 1) _____,
   2) _____, 3) _____, & 4) _____.

5. Look up Map. What page does it start on? _____
   List three kinds of people you see using maps:
   1) _____, 2) _____, & 3) _____.

#2   *Finding a fact*

Concepts
1. Entries are arranged alphabetically.
2. Guide words at top or bottom of page help in locating entry.
3. A fact is a single piece of information about a topic.
4. An entry includes many facts about the topic.

Materials
A set of general encyclopedias.
A worksheet.

Procedures
1. Select topics with entries of one or two paragraphs only.
2. Make up a worksheet which asks the students to locate the entry and to write one fact from the entry in their own words. (Sample worksheet is based on *World Book Encyclopedia*.)
3. Present concepts to students.
4. Hand out worksheets.
5. Provide help as needed.

Student Products
Completed worksheet.

Time Commitment
Probably one week would be adequate.

Adaptations
Look up the same topic in another encyclopedia. If found, see if the same fact appears in that entry.

Encyclopedia Worksheet #2

Look up each of the topics listed below. Read the entry. Find one fact. Write it in your own words. Do Not Copy the Entry. Include the volume and page number where you found the fact.

1. Beeswax Vol. ____ Page____ Fact _____

_____

_____

2. Fathom Vol. ____ Page____ Fact _____

_____

_____

3. Lemur Vol. ____ Page____ Fact _____

_____

_____

4. Trilobite Vol. ____ Page____ Fact _____

_____

_____

#3   *Thematic find a specific fact*

Concepts
1. Entries are arranged alphabetically.
2. Guide words at top or bottom of page help in locating entry.
3. A fact is a single piece of information about a topic.
4. An entry includes many facts about the topic.

Materials
A set of general encyclopedias.
A set of questions on a theme.

Procedures
1. Select a theme such as snow, water, people, food, etc.
2. Make up a set of questions about topics related to the chosen theme. Questions should ask for a specific fact.
3. Review concepts with students.
4. Let students begin.
5. Provide help as needed.

Student Product
Answers to the questions.

Time Commitment
Probably one week would be adequate.

Adaptations
Give students a theme and let them develop a set of questions. Sets of questions could then be swapped and answered.

Sample questions: Do You Snow the Answer?
1. Is an iceberg made of fresh or salt water? Is there more showing above or below the water?
2. What is an ice breaker? What is the name of the biggest one?
3. What is the best type of snowplow to use to clear deep drifts? How does it work?
4. Did children during the Civil War have coasting sleds? When did they come into use in the United States?
5. No two snowflakes are just alike, but all snowflakes have the same number of sides. How many sides does a snowflake have?
6. The record for the biggest snowfall for a twenty-four hour period was set in what year, in what city, and left how much snow?
7. What is a snowdrop?

8. What were the first skis made of? What are modern skis made of?
9. Why does wearing snowshoes keep you from sinking into deep snow as you walk?
10. What is sometimes used as a window in an igloo?

Concepts

1. Using subheadings saves time.
2. Subheadings are identifiable by style and size of type, and by placement on the page.
3. Subheadings help one locate specific information within a large amount of print.

Materials

A general encyclopedia that uses subheadings within articles. (*World Book Encyclopedia* is used for the examples that follow.) A set of questions based on the references to be used.

Procedures

1. Select an article with a number of subheadings such as *Christmas* or the *Circus*.
2. Develop questions related to the various subheadings used.
3. Write questions on 3x5 cards or on a worksheet.
4. Number the questions.
5. Explain usefulness of subheadings to students.
6. Display cards or distribute worksheet.

Student Products

Completed answer sheet.

Time Commitment

One week should be sufficient.

Adaptations

Students could be asked to create questions related to subheads in an assigned article(s). These questions could then be answered by classmates.

Sample Questions

Questions related to subheadings for *World Book* article on Christmas Customs:

1. What are Italians' favorite foods to eat at Christmas time?
2. In Finland what do they do for the birds?
3. What is the main dish served for Christmas dinner in Sweden?
4. What do fountains have to do with Christmas celebrations in Switzerland?
5. Who were the first people to use Christmas tree decorations?

Questions related to *World Book* article on the Circus:
1. What might you see in a side show?
2. What do the circus winter quarters look like?
3. What were circus tents called?
4. How many large circuses toured the United States in the late 1800s?
5. What do you call the men who unload the equipment and set it up?

Specialized References

As interest and demands of assignments expand, students need to be introduced to a variety of specialized references. They should develop awareness of and skill in using these materials to augment the use of general encyclopedias.

#1 *Atlas activity for Hallowe'en*

Concepts
1. The need to use the index to find information in an atlas.
2. Indexes are arranged alphabetically.
3. Subheadings are indicated by indentions or change in type face.

Materials
An atlas to be used by the teacher in constructing the worksheet. Worksheets for each student.

Procedures
1. Construct worksheet which asks students to identify the state in which towns with a Hallowe'en connotation are located.
2. A modified index is constructed for use in answering the worksheet questions.
3. This index includes a list of ten towns for each state in which the Hallowe'en town name is located. (See sample.)

Student Products
Completed answer sheet.

Time Commitment
One class period.

Adaptations
Have the students choose a town name from the sample index and, using their imaginations, create a story telling how this town got its name.

Town names related to another theme such as people, things, a season, or rhyming names could be used.

Sample Worksheet

ATLAS ACTIVITY

It might seem like Hallowe'en all year if you lived in one of these towns. Beside each town, write the name of the state in which it is found.

1. Bigwitch Gap _____
2. Devils Dish _____
3. Dread and Terror Ridge _____
4. Goblin Valley _____
5. Monsterville _____
6. Mummy Cave _____
7. Skeleton Springs _____
8. Skull Point _____
9. Tombstone _____
10. Water Witch _____

Use the following Index to find your answers:

Al ASKA
Anchorage
Buckland
Devils Dish
Fairbanks
Goodnews
King Cove
Moose Pass
Nome
Pelican
Skagway

ARIZONA
Big Field
Buckeye
Christmas
Flagstaff
Grand Canyon
Parks
Phoenix
Sun City

Tombstone
Window Rock

CALIFORNIA
Anaheim
Big Pine
Hood
Los Angeles
Monsterville
Palm Springs
San Francisco
Yosemite Junction

COLORADO
Baxter
Boulder
Crook
Denver
Estes Park
Lake City
Leadville

Rifle
Silt
Skull Point

NEW JERSEY
Bayonne
Cherry Hill
Edgewater
Livingston
Newark
Perth Amboy
Rockaway
Tenafly
Trenton
Water Witch

NORTH CAROLINA
Bigwitch Gap
Blowing Rock
Buxton
Chapel Hill

Elm City
Hatteras
Kitty Hawk
Liberty
Old Trap
Weeksville

OREGON

Beaver
Cloverdale
Deer Island
Dread and Terror
 Ridge
Echo
Fossil
Kings Valley
Newberg

SOUTH DAKOTA
Buffalo Gap
Deadwood
Freeman
Hot Springs
Keystone
Lead
Pickstown
Skeleton Spring
Spearfish
Woonsocket

UTAH
Bonanza
Goblin Valley
Helper
Hurricane

Lark
Minersville
Oakley
Paradise
Salt Lake City
Woodruff

WYOMING
Laramie
Linch
Medicine Bow
Mummy Cave
Osage
Pine Bluff
Story
Sunrise
Ten Sleep
Upton

Choose a town name from the index and write a story telling how
the town got its name. Use your imagination.

#2   With an atlas index

Concepts
1. Indexes are arranged alphabetically.
2. An atlas index gives additional information such as population, location of a town on the map, paging to find the map, state name, etc.
3. The same name can be used for a river, county, mountain, or town.
4. The letter and number coordinates refer to the grid designations on the map.
5. Names of towns can also be common words with everyday meanings.

Materials
Atlases with a unified alphabetical index. (Not broken down by states or regions.)
Question sheet.

Procedures
1. Create questions based on examination of atlas index.
2. Select town names which have common everyday meanings.
3. Phrase a question related to this everyday meaning.
4. Construct worksheet.
5. Include in the directions the types of information wanted in the answer, i.e., population, state, grid coordinates.
6. Distribute worksheet.
7. Do additional sample questions for use in demonstration.
8. Provide atlases.

Student Products
Completed worksheet.

Time Commitment
Determined by number of students and number of available atlases.

Adaptations
Have students make up additional questions following the same format.
Share questions and answers.

Sample Questions

WHAT TOWN NAME IS THE SAME AS:

1. a piece of clothing? (Hood, California)
2. an animal? (Beaver, Oregon)
3. a bird? (Pelican, Alaska)
4. an old TV show? (Bonanza, Utah)
5. a new TV show? (Dallas, Texas)
6. a tree? (Elm City, North Carolina)
7. what the American Revolution was fought for? (Liberty, North Carolina)
8. a kind of storm? (Hurricane, Utah)
9. to hang someone without a trial? (Lynch, Maryland)
10. something that happens each morning? (Sunrise, Wyoming)
11. a kind of seafood dish? (Newberg, Oregon)
12. when sound bounces back? (Echo, Oregon)
13. a big rock? (Boulder, Colorado)
14. someone who assists someone else? (Helper, Utah)
15. another name for heaven? (Paradise, Utah)
16. a sport? (Spearfish, South Dakota)
17. the outline of a plant or animal in stone? (Fossil, Oregon)
18. a villain? (Crook, Colorado)
19. a kind of weapon? (Rifle, Colorado)
20. the name of an African explorer? (Livingston, New Jersey)

Try to make up additional questions yourself.

Give name of state, population, and map grid information for the town whose name means the same as each of the above.

#3 Trace a name across the U.S.A.

Concepts
1. Place names reflect the migration of people.
2. The same name is used in various locales.

Materials
Outline map of the U.S. for each student.
Atlases of the U.S.

Procedures
1. Select a list of town names which recur several times across the U.S. (for instance, Columbus or Madison)
2. Discuss with students the concept of naming places, and how people often take names along with them when they move.
3. Hand out outline maps of the U.S.A.
4. Assign a town name to each student.
5. Ask students to plot on their map the places where that town name appears.
6. Connect these locations with a line to show east-west migration and progression.

Student Products
Completed map for assigned town name.

Time Commitment
One week.

Adaptations
Look into the origin of the town name, the original town's location (possibly a place in a foreign country for which American towns are named), dates of settlement, or other pertinent information.

Specialized dictionaries activity

Concepts

1. Unabridged dictionaries do not contain all the words in our language.
2. Dictionaries exist which are related to specific topics and subjects.
3. Analyze the question for clue words which will direct one's choice of dictionary.

Materials

Collection of specialized dictionaries such as foreign language, scientific, nursery rhyme, mythological, biographical, geographical, etc.

Set of questions using the available specialized dictionaries in the collection.

Procedures

1. Determine what dictionaries are available.
2. Write questions which require the use of these references.
3. Hold discussion with participating students about dictionaries, their similarities and differences, arrangements, purposes, and unique characteristics and arrangements.
4. Hand out worksheets and let students begin.

Student Products

Completed worksheet.

Time Commitment

One week.

Adaptations

Have students bring in specialized dictionaries they have at home to learn that a wide range of specialized dictionaries exists.

Sample Questions

SPECIALIZED DICTIONARIES

For each question write the title of the book you found the answer in and the page number where you found the answer. If you want to answer the question as well go ahead.

1. What is the definition of the word integer?

2. Who was Jupiter?

3. The French word bonbon means what in English?
4. The word in Spanish for fire engine is what?
5. What part of the plant is the bracteole?
6. What is an animal's thorax?
7. In the nursery rhyme, what was the hobby horse's tail made of?
8. What is a synonym for the word macabre?
9. Where in the world is Kailua Bay?
10. Who was William Murdock?
11. What does it mean to be called a "dead ringer" for someone?

The more you do, the better, but a minimum of six is required.

Acronyms activity

Concepts

1. Certain words in our language are a series of letters standing for individual words; e.g., UNESCO, NATO. These words appear in all capital letters.
2. There are certain other words in our language which are not capitalized and are also derived from the initial letters of words in a phrase; e.g., tips (to insure prompt service); scuba (self-contained underwater breathing apparatus); or news (north, east, west, south).

Materials

Acronym dictionaries.
Phrase and word origin books.

Procedures

1. Discuss the concept of acronyms with students.
2. Share some examples of acronyms with students.
3. Have students discover additional examples to share with the group.

Student Products

A bulletin board list of contributions.

Time Commitment

Two weeks, or more if interest has not waned.

Adaptations

Clip examples of these expressions from newspapers and magazines and post them on the bulletin board.

Biographical dictionary of fictional book characters

Concepts
1. Concept of collected biography vs. individual biography.
2. Dictionary will be arranged alphabetically.
3. Dictionaries of fictional characters list entries by last name if it is well known, others by first name.

Materials
Fiction collection to provide reading selections.
Biographical dictionary.
Fictional character dictionary, such as *Dictionary of Fictional Characters* by Freeman or *Readers Handbook* by Brewer.
Format sheet dittoed for student use.

Procedures
1. Explain the concept of collected biography as found in biographical dictionaries.
2. Point out similarity between biography of real people and identification of fictional characters.
3. Suggest that the group construct a dictionary with entries being "biographies" of characters in the fiction books the students are currently reading. (Avoid duplication of character, although several characters could come from the same book.)
4. Provide a format sheet for each character being included in the "dictionary."
5. Student turns in completed "biography," and teacher compiles the loose-leaf book.

Student Products
Completed format sheet(s).

Time Commitment
About two weeks.

Adaptations
Have students continue to add characters and expand the "dictionary" as additional books are read.

Sample Worksheet

FICTIONAL CHARACTER DICTIONARY ENTRY

Character's name _____

Title of book _____
          (Could use poem, play, or movie)

Author _____

Setting (time and place)

_____

_____

Description of character:

   Age _____

   Appearance _____

   _____

   Personality traits _____

   _____

   _____

   Adventures (accomplishments, problems, disasters, etc.)

   _____

   _____

   _____

Contemporaries activity

Concepts

1. Contemporaries are people whose lifetimes are concurrent.
2. "Contemporary" does not always mean "modern" or "the present." Julius Caesar and George Washington had contemporaries in their lifetimes.

Materials

The book *Who Was When* or other concordances that list people. Additional biographical references that provide birth and death dates.

List of people's names for students to look up.

Procedures

1. Using the reference materials at hand, develop a list of individuals for students to categorize as contemporaries.
2. Discuss with students the concept of contemporaries and the resources available to the students.
3. Hand out list of names to students. Directions ask students to identify individuals by profession and nationality, and to group them according to life spans.

Student Products

A chart of contemporaries.

Time Commitment

Influenced by length of list of names and availability of materials. Probably one to two weeks.

Adaptations

Names could be placed on a time-line type of chart.

Sample Worksheet

I. Give the profession, nationality, and life span of each of the following:

Name	Profession	Nationality	Life span
1. _____	_____	_____	_____
2. _____	_____	_____	_____
3. _____	_____	_____	_____
4. _____	_____	_____	_____

II. Classify individuals as contemporaries; i.e., make lists of people who were alive at the same time.

Examples of Names Which Could Be Used:

Bell, Alexander G.	1847-1922
Burr, Aaron	1756-1836
Dante, Alighieri	1265-1322
Edison, Thomas	1847-1931
Lincoln, Abraham	1809-1865
Marie Antoinette	1755-1793
Mozart, Wolfgang A.	1756-1791
Polo, Marco	1254-1323
Twain, Mark	1835-1910
Woolworth, Frank W.	1852-1919

Around the year with poetry

Concepts

1. Poetry often uses themes related to seasons.
2. There are indexes to help locate poems on specific themes.
3. Collections of poetry are often arranged by theme or subject. (These are more useful for this project than a book of poems by one author.)

Materials

Granger's Index to Poetry
Index to Children's Poetry
Various collections of poetry arranged by theme or subject; such as *Poetry for Pleasure, Boy's Book of Verse,* or *A Way of Knowing.*

Procedures

1. Introduce the use of poetry indexes.
2. Introduce the use of poetry collections arranged by theme.
3. Ask students to select a poem suitable for each month of the year, and to make a calendar pairing the poetry with the appropriate month.
4. Illustrations could accompany poetry on calendar pages.

Student Products

Completed calendar.

Time Commitment

One marking period.

Adaptations

Do just one month tied in with a special holiday such as Mother's Day, Father's Day, Hallowe'en, Christmas, etc.

Calendar of famous firsts or unusual events

Concepts

1. Some calendars include information about special days.
2. Weeks are set aside to recognize certain activities; e.g., National Library Week, Fire Prevention Week, or American Education Week.
3. Days are designated to remember individuals or events; e.g., Martin Luther King Day, Secretary's Day, Groundhog Day.
4. There are more events than days in the year, so some days carry multiple designations.

Materials

Famous First Facts by Kane
Guinness Book of Records
Other books of "firsts".

Procedures

1. Make a ditto of calendar pages for the year making each day's square large enough for the student to write in a famous "first" that occured on that date.
2. Discuss the concepts listed above.
3. Discuss how to use the reference books available.
4. Hand out calendar pages and have students begin project.

Student Products

Completed calendar.

Time Commitment

One marking period.

Adaptations

Could do a single month such as the one including the student's birthday.

Could divide students into four teams and have each team do a season of three months.

Specialized reference books: Overview

Concepts
1. Specialized references related to specific topics provide more in-depth and detailed information about a topic than do general references.
2. Recognize the clues within the question which direct one to the specific reference to be used.
3. Identify special reference books within the collection.

Materials
A wide collection of specialized reference books.
A set of questions derived from these books.

Procedures
1. Determine which books within the reference collection will be used for this project.
2. Devise a set of questions requiring the use of these books.
3. Present the individual characteristics of the reference books to the students.
4. Analyze sample questions to indicate how to match questions and reference book needed.
   For example, question number 5 on the accompanying worksheet, "Frances Willard was a famous American. Find a picture of her. What is she doing?" can be analyzed to provide the following clues: *American, female, picture.* Given the choices of reference books provided at the end of the question sheet, a picture of an American female would most likely be found in *Pictorial History of Women in America.*
5. Hand out worksheet and let students proceed.

Student Products
Completed worksheet giving factual answer, title and page number of book where answer was actually found.

Time Commitment
Probably about two weeks depending on size of reference collection and number of questions asked.

Adaptations
Additional questions could be placed on file cards kept in a file box, and available as an on-going challenge for use whenever the student wants to try to find an answer. Post one question as "Question of the Day".

Sample Worksheet

SPECIALIZED REFERENCE BOOKS

Use the materials in your reference collection to answer the following questions. For each item answer the question and cite the page and title where you found the answer.

1. When and of what was the children's book character Hitty made?
2. On March 23 of what year was the first patent issued for a rivet? Name something else that happened for the first time in that year.
3. What had Hermes, the gods' messenger, done by noon of the day he was born?
4. Which presidents lived to be 90 or older?
5. Frances Willard was a famous American. Find a picture of her. What is she doing?
6. Who was the sculptor who made the Statue of Liberty?
7. Do men or women perform the scalp dance?
8. Find an illustration of a two-stroke diesel engine.
9. What city seemed to set the style for men's clothing during the years 1900–1910?
10. In a nursery rhyme, what was the hobby horse's tail made of?
11. What is the average annual salary of a funeral director?
12. Find a page-long definition of the scientific term mitochondria.
13. What is the symbol for the mathematical term square root?
14. Find a picture of a fossil of a bony fish. In what state was it found?
15. Are Japanese beetles found in New England?
16. What was one factor leading to the technological improvements in road building?
17. What is the first thing you do if you are going to serve southern-fried catfish?
18. During the Renaissance many great churches were built. How long did it take to build St. Peter's Basilica?
19. McCloskey has won two Caldecott medals for his illustrations of childrens' books. In what years did he win the award?
20. There have been a number of musical prodigies. At the age of four this flute player was supporting his family. Who was he?
21. How many Academy Awards did Walt Disney win in 1954?

22. In what anthology of poems will you find the poem "No One Cares Less Than I" by Edward Thomas?
23. What is the oldest city in Nicaragua? When was it founded?
24. Find a map of the United States as it was in 1910.
25. Find reproductions of newspaper stories telling of the California gold rush of 1849.
26. What did Roberto Moranzoni do for a living?
27. How many children did Scott Corbett have?
28. List three words that mean the same as hash when hash is used as a noun meaning mixture.
29. Who was voted into the Hall of Fame for Great Americans in 1955?
30. What are the French and Spanish words that mean Monday?

In developing these questions the following books were used:

Album of American History
Webster's Biographical Dictionary
Something About the Author
Roget's Thesaurus
Information Please Almanac
French and Spanish Dictionaries
Oxford Dictionary of Nursery Rhymes
Handbook of Job Facts
More Words of Science
Mathematics Dictionary
Fossil Book
Atlas of Insects
History of Technology
Joy of Cooking
Renaissance
Granger's Index to Poetry
Land and People Encyclopedia
Oxford Junior Companion to Music
Art of Walt Disney
Shepard's Historical Atlas
Who's Who in Children's Books
Famous First Facts
Dictionary of Mythology
Facts About the Presidents
Pictorial History of Women in America
What so Proudly We Hail
American Indians
Complete Junior Encyclopedia of Transportation
Five Centuries of American Costume
Illustrators of Books for Young People

Skills used with Report Writing

The ability to write a high quality report is dependent upon the development of a set of skills. This does not happen without guidance and instruction as well as practice. When initial report-writing assignments are made, the assignments should require the use of an outline, note cards, and correct bibliographic forms. Skills, once developed, should continue to be required.

Outlining activity

Concepts
1. Outlines are arranged in a sequential order moving from general to specific.
2. A standard symbolic format is used in outlining: Roman numerals, capital letters, Arabic numerals, small letters.
3. Topics of similar importance or value will be represented by the same type of symbol.

Materials
Worksheets.

Procedures
1. Assemble a collection of terms related to a topic. Include in the set one over-all term for the title, several large subtopics, and specifics related to each subtopic.
2. Present words in "mixed-up" order. (See sample.)
3. Construct worksheet.
4. Discuss with students the structure of an outline.
5. Do a few sample outlines for practice as a group.
6. Hand out worksheet and have students proceed.

Student Products
Completed worksheet.

Time Commitment
Basically one class session with follow-up as needed.

Adaptations
Have students choose a topic and develop a set of terms demonstrating the relationship of general to specific.

Sample Worksheet

OUTLINING: GENERAL TO SPECIFIC

1.
North America   Provinces   Cities
States   Mexico   Canada   States
United States   Cities   Cities

2.
Trees   Broadleaf   Pine   Cedar   Palm
Conifer   Oak   Date   Coconut   Maple

3.
Animals Nonpoisonous Land Sea Birds Mammals
Reptiles   With Flight   Without Flight   Poisonous

4.
Air   Submarines   Gliders   Trains   Transportation
Cars   Land   Trucks   Sea   Ocean Liners   Sailboats
Airplanes   Blimps

Fit these sets of words into this outline format.

I. _____

  A. _____

     1. _____

     2. _____

     3. _____

  B. _____

     1. _____

     2. _____

     3. _____

  C. _____

     1. _____

     2. _____

     3. _____

Skimming for specific information #1

Concepts
1. It is not necessary to read an entire book to locate a fact.
2. Subheadings, picture captions, chapter headings are important sources of information when the specific fact needed in order to use the index is unknown.
3. Analysis of question provides clues to use in the search.

Materials
Set of books on subtopics related to a field of interest; e.g., Lerner's series.
Set of questions calling for a specific fact from each book not readily identifiable through the index.

Procedures
1. Develop a set of questions by skimming the books paying particular attention to photo captions, subheadings, etc.
2. Pick facts that will be of interest but are not likely to be known ahead of time.
3. Prepare ditto sheet of questions.
4. Place books on reserve to assure access.
5. Present project to group and allow time for completion.

Student Products
Completed answer sheet.

Time Commitment
Anything from a single class period to a week's time.

Adaptations
Assignment can be completed by an individual or can be structured for team competition. If competition is wanted, have multiple sets of materials so that each team has its own set. Winning team is the one which requires the least amount of time to locate all answers.

Sample Worksheet

Using the *In America* series by Lerner, fill in the blanks giving the name of the country from which the person or the person's ancestors emigrated:

1. (Greece, p. 64) — Designer of the Brooklyn Bridge.
2. (France, p. 88) — Inventor of the semi-automatic rifle used by the U.S. Army during WWI.
3. (Hungary, p. 56) — Man who isolated and identified Vitamin C.
4. (Sweden, p. 41) — Founder of the Greyhound Bus Line.
5. (E. India, p. 54) — Youngest conductor ever to lead a major symphony orchestra.
6. (Mexico, p. 93) — Pro golfer named sportsman of the year in 1971.
7. (Scotland, p. 77) — Naturalist who helped establish national parks. (John Muir)
8. (Ukraine, p. 84) — Immigrants who have been guided by the motto "Absorb all cultures but forget not your own."
9. (Russia, p. 83) — Immigrants who have known special preeminence in the art of the dance.
10. (China, p. 89) — Highest paid cameraman in Hollywood who has won Oscars for *Hud* and *The Rose Tattoo*.
11. (Italy, p. 35) — Founder of the Chun King Corporation.
12. (Netherlands, p. 84) — Gave America 49 carillon bells in gratitude for aid given during WWII.
13. (Poland, p. 66) — Woman largely responsible for the renewed interest in the harpsichord and its music.
14. (Japan, p. 66) — Nationality which comprises the single largest ethnic group in Hawaii.
15. (Czechoslovakia, p. 67) — Architect who designed the gothic spires of St. Patrick's Cathedral in NYC.
16. (Ireland, p. 46) — Song writers Victor Herbert and George M. Cohan.

Skimming for specific information #2

Concepts
1. It is not necessary to read an entire book to locate a fact.
2. Use of tables of contents or indexes can help locate specific information.
3. Table of contents is arranged in page order and index is arranged in alphabetic order.
4. The question contains key words which may be used in either table of contents or index.

Materials
A collection of biographies found in school library media center.
A set of questions the answers to which can be found through the use of either the table of contents or indexes of these books.

Procedures
1. Select a group of biographies at an appropriate reading level which contain a table of contents and/or index.
2. Create a set of questions by locating interesting facts through the use of the table of contents or index.
3. Arrange questions on a worksheet giving the biographee's name followed by the question about the person.
4. Place books on a reserve shelf.
5. Distribute worksheets.
6. Discuss efficient ways of finding the answers using additional samples.

Student Products
Completed answer sheet.

Time Commitment
One to two weeks should be adequate.

Adaptations
Could be structured as a contest by dividing the class into teams. The winner could be selected based on finishing first, or by winning in a quiz show format scheduled later.

Sample Worksheet

SKIM TO FIND THE ANSWERS

1. James Beckworth—What happened that made him become a mountain man?
2. Frederic Douglass—How did he learn to read and write?
3. Harriet Tubman—What did she do that most runaway slaves didn't do?
4. Robert Smalls—How did he gain his freedom?
5. Booker T. Washington—What was the purpose of his school in Tuskegee?
6. Sojourner Truth—What two movements did she work with? What did president Lincoln show her?
7. Jan Matzeliger—What did the machine he invented do?
8. Nat Love—How did he get the money to become a cowboy?
9. Sacajawea—Name three ways she helped Lewis and Clark.
10. Tecumseh—When he began to unite the Indian tribes Governor Harrison asked him to perform a miracle. What did he do?
11. Sitting Bull—What were his greatest assets as a leader?
12. Chief Joseph—He didn't want to fight, but was forced to. What made him surrender? Did the white settlers treat the Indians honorably?
13. Narcissa Whitman—Why is she remembered? How did she die?
14. Mary Walker—What was her interest in animals?
15. Abigail Scott—What made her become a suffragette?
16. Susan B. Anthony—What was the word she didn't want included in the constitution?
17. Clara Barton—What was one of the disasters the American Red Cross sent help to?
18. Andrew Carnegie—In what industry did he become the richest man in the world? What was one reason for his success?
19. James Watt—What did he invent? Find where Watt tells how he got the idea for a separate condenser.
20. Samuel Slater—How was the first textile machinery built? Why?
21. Eli Whitney—What was his first invention? He also developed the twin principles of modern production. What are they?
22. Robert Fulton—Did he really invent the first steamboat? If not, why is he remembered?
23. Cyrus McCormick—He is remembered for inventing a workable reaper. What did such a machine have to be able to do?

24. Gail Borden—He said, "I will be remembered as the inventor of a great process." What was he referring to?
25. Charles Goodyear—In 1839 Goodyear accidently discovered what process?
26. Henry Bessemer—He developed a process for making better iron. How did he test his new iron?
27. Edwin Drake—Who was the real father of the petroleum industry Bissell, Drake, or Townsend? What did each of these men do?
28. Thomas Edison—His deafness may have dated from an explosion when one of his experiments caught fire. What are two versions of the story?
29. Wright Brothers—How many reporters were there when they made their first flight? Where did it take place?
30. Alexander Graham Bell—What did he give his wife for a wedding present?
31. Allen Pinkerton—How did he get into the private detective business? He hired the first woman detective. Who was she?
32. Walter Reed—How did he find the cause of yellow fever or "yellow jack" as it was called?
33. John James Audubon—Because of his ambition he seldom let a day go by without drawing. What was his ambition?
34. Johnny Appleseed—What was his real name? How did he get his nickname?
35. Samuel Clemens—What was his pen name? What does it mean?
36. General Custer—What was his last plan to get away from the Indians? Describe the scene when he died. Who was with him?

Use the books on the book truck in your classroom to answer these questions. Use the table of contents and index to help locate the information asked for. Skim to find the answers.

Sample

DIRECTIONS FOR QUIZ SHOW ADAPTATION

Your final activity will be a contest patterned after "It's Academic". Each class will be divided into two teams. Each team will be divided into part A and part B, with a captain for each. Nine questions will be asked of team I part A. Nine questions will be asked of Team II part A. If one team cannot answer the question the other team will be given a chance. Five points will be scored for each correct answer. At the end of round one the A parts of team I and team II will be replaced by the B parts. A second round of nine questions will be asked each of these groups. The total score for team I and team II will determine the winner. If an answer is called out from the audience the team members who called out will have ten points subtracted from their score. The first answer given by a team will count. Talk it over before you speak out. Perhaps you should let the captain speak for the team. Good luck to all of you.

Bibliographic forms

Concepts
1. Research reports should include a bibliography of references used in preparing the report.
2. A consistent form should be used.
3. There is a variety of accepted styles that may be used, but one of these will be selected and applied consistently.
4. Regardless of the bibliographic form used, the following information appears in a bibliography: Author, title, publisher, place of publishing, date of publishing, and pages used.
5. Bibliographic entries are arranged in alphabetic order.

Materials
A style sheet (commercial or teacher made) to be used by the students. Either a collection of materials to serve as examples or the needed information reproduced on a ditto or transparency.

Procedures
1. Discuss what a bibliography is and why is it included in a paper.
2. Identify the parts of bibliographic entries and where the entries are found in materials used.
3. Explain that there are various acceptable bibliographic formats and present the one that will be used in this assignment.
4. Use a number of common examples for group practices. (Ditto or transparency providing necessary information).

   Example:

   A book of photographic puns called *Punography Too* was written by Bruce A. McMillan. Penguin Books of New York published it in 1980.
5. Verify correctness of student responses in terms of sequence of elements and punctuation.
6. When students have mastered format for a book, present format for an encyclopedia article.
7. Verify mastery by having students write a bibliographic entry for an item.
8. As a group, alphabetize these into a single bibliography.

Student Products
Practice sheets for common examples.
Entry for group bibliography.
Bibliographies included in appropriate future assignments.

Time Commitment

A single class period with additional practice if necessary.

Adaptations

Master format for other types of materials including nonprint items, periodicals, interviews, letters, microforms, etc.

Examples for Group Practice:

John Hoke wrote a book called The First Book of Snakes. It was published by Franklin Watts Inc. in New York in 1956. Rattlesnakes are discussed on pages 42–45.

World Book has an article on rattlesnakes on pages 144–146 of Vol. 16 It was written by Clifford Pope. The encyclopedia was published by Field Enterprises in Chicago in 1977.

The World of Snakes was written by Hal Harrison and published by Lippincott Co. in Philadelphia in 1971. Rattlesnakes are presented on pages 82–89.

Vol. 9 of Grolier's Amazing World of Animals gives information about rattlesnakes on pages 136–140 in the article called "Pit Vipers-Cratalidae."

(On this sheet titles of books are not underlined so as to avoid giving clues.)

Thematic report writing using a common outline

Concepts

1. Use of an outline to structure the report *before* search is started.
2. Notes should be taken on cards, one idea per card, and keyed to the outline.
3. Note taking involves selecting key words and phrases, not copying complete sentences or paragraphs.
4. Information is taken from more than one source.
5. A bibliography is a part of a report and is written according to a standard form.
6. Rough draft is written before the final draft, and improvements are made.

Materials

Basic reference collection.
Basic nonfiction collection.
Outline for student use in this project.
Note cards cut from scrap paper.
Bibliographic style sheet.

Procedures

1. Select a topic that has enough subtopics that each student has a different and specific one. Examples are countries, states, animals, chemical elements, sports, etc.
2. Develop an outline related to the general topic which can be applied to each specific topic.
3. Teach students to write correct bibliographic form.
4. Teach students to take notes and to key note cards to outline.
5. Give each student an outline and a trade book on a subtopic; e.g., Carpenter's *State* books, *Land and People* series, or a book from a similar series on some topic.
6. Review with students the terminology used on the outline so they know the type of information they are looking for.
7. Discuss time-line for the assignment and point out that one topic on the outline is to be completed (i.e., note cards, rough draft, final draft) before beginning this process for the next topic. (See sample.)
8. Have students begin the research project.

Student Products

Note cards, rough drafts, and a finished report including a bibliography.

Time Commitment

Approximately one week per topic on the outline preceded by however much instruction time is required to launch the project. This will vary with skill level and experience of students.

Adaptations

Additional requirements in terms of a project cover, table of contents, illustrations, etc. as desired by the teacher. Additional topics could be used such as authors, musicians, inventors, explorers, industries, vegetables, trees, insects, rocks, etc.

Sample Outline

COMMON OUTLINE FOR RESEARCH REPORTS

Country _____

I. Land
   A. Location and size
   B. Surface features
   C. Climate
II. Resources
   A. Natural resources
   B. Manufacturing
   C. Agriculture
III. History
IV. Government
V. People
   A. Education
   B. Culture
      1. language
      2. money
      3. dress
      4. festivals
VI. Bibliography
   A. Land and People book
   B. General Encyclopedia
   C. Social Studies Encyclopedia

Directions for country report:
1. For each topic on the outline you will turn in note cards, a rough draft, and the final copy.
2. Topic I is due _____ .
   Topic II is due _____ .
   Topic III is due _____ .
   Topic IV is due _____ .
   Topic V is due _____ .
   Topic VI is due _____ .
   Compiled finished copy with bibliography is due _____ .
3. Your notes will consist of key words and phrases. Do not copy complete sentences.
4. Your rough draft will be written from your note cards.

5. Bibliographic form for a book:
     Last Name, First; *Title*; Publisher,
     Place, Date, Pages.
6. Bibliographic form for an encyclopedia:
     Last Name, First; "Article"; *Title of Enc.*
     Publisher, Place, Date.
     Volume, Pages.

Curriculum-related Activities

Activities that are made a part of ongoing classroom activity have greater meaning for students than those that occur unrelated to the rest of their curriculum. Practical application for the search skills introduced earlier is found in curriculum-related projects. Social studies and literature units provide most readily for the application of such skills.

Conducting a poll on a topic of concern

Concepts
1. A questionnaire is a tool used to assess opinion.
2. The wording and format of a questionnaire can influence the outcome of the survey.
3. Care must be used to design a bias-free questionnaire.
4. The questionnaire should be piloted and revised as needed before being used in the survey.

Materials
Sample questionnaires from various surveys to illustrate possible formats.

Procedures
1. Select examples of questionnaires to be shared with students.
2. Discuss an issue of concern with the students, and through discussion decide upon developing a questionnaire to use in examining this concern.
3. Have students look at samples to see the range of questionnaire format.
4. Have students develop a list of information sought.
5. Have students develop questions to be used in the questionnaire.
6. Test and revise questionnaires as needed. (This could be done several times.)
7. Create final questionnaire.
8. Identify population to be questioned.
9. Administer questionnaire to desired population.
10. Tabulate results.

Student Products
Group's questionnaire.
Tally sheets.

Time Commitment
One month to marking period.

Adaptations
Manipulate the wording of a single question in an attempt to influence the answers given. Use two or three versions of the question in order to compare results.

Sample wordings of questions might be the following:
   A. The Bond Issue should be passed.
   B. The Bond Issue which will aid the poor of the city should be passed.
   C. Although taxes will need to be raised, the Bond Issue should be passed.

School-wide postal system

Concepts
1. Importance of an accurate address.
2. Steps involved in collecting, sorting, and delivering mail.
3. Mail is picked up and delivered on a schedule.

Materials
A supply of letters written by students and staff to other students and staff within the building.
A receptacle in which to collect mail.
Boxes for sorting mail.
Daily schedule from each classroom indicating the most convenient time to deliver mail.

Procedures
1. Decorate and label receptacle for mail collection.
2. Label boxes into which mail is sorted.
3. Assign duties to members of the group involved in the activity: sorters, letter carriers.
4. Establish a delivery schedule and routes based on classroom schedules.
5. Make an announcement that service is now functioning.
6. Encourage teachers to have students participate, possibly through assigned letter writing.

Student Products
Delivered mail.

Time Commitment
As long as interest supports the project.

Adaptations
Use for Valentine's Day cards; return of overdue library items.

Collect postmarks

Concepts
1. There is a postmark on each piece of mail put there by the post office at which it is mailed.
2. Each of these locations can be identified geographically and can be found on a map.
3. The words on the postmark include names of cities, states, and countries.

Materials
Large scale outline map of the United States and/or the world.
Collection of postmarks.
Collection of atlases and road maps.

Procedures
1. Enlarge outline map to be bulletin board size. (Use opaque projector.)
2. Have students bring in postmarks cut from envelopes.
3. Have students locate on the map the appropriate position for the postmark using atlases and maps as necessary.

Student Products
To bring in the postmark, identify the locale, and place the postmark in its proper position on the map.

Time Commitment
A few minutes a day for as long as the project holds the attention of the group.

Adaptations
Depending on the location of the bulletin board used, it can involve either a class or the entire school.

Can be an appropriate nonreligious activity for the December holidays since mail is received in greater volume and from a wider variety of locations.

Can be used as a statewide study unit.

Create a hall of fame

Concepts
1. Hall of fame inductees are chosen because they are the outstanding individuals in their field.
2. Halls of fame exist for a variety of fields.

Materials
Biographical reference collection.
Books on Halls of Fame.

Procedures
1. Discuss the concept of a Hall of Fame with the group and elicit examples from students' backgrounds.
2. Explain that each student will create a list of ten inductees for a hall of fame in a field of their choice (to be approved by the teacher.) Possible fields for halls of fame might be inventors, explorers, mountain climbers, composers, artists, comedians, dancers, medical researchers or child prodigies.
3. In addition to listing the names, justification for including the individual selected must be provided.

Student Products
A series of ten paper "plaques," one for each inductee.
Wording on the "plaques" will include inductee's name, dates, and contributions to the field.

Time Commitment
About a month. Most of the time will be spent in evaluating and reading about the people for possible inclusion.
About a week will be needed to make the "plaques."

Adaptations
Create a "Good Deeds Hall of Fame," selecting members from the current school population.

Read your way around the world

Concepts
1. Stories are set in different countries.
2. The exact geographic setting influences the story.

Materials
Outline map of the world for each student (11x17).
A fiction collection that includes stories set in different countries.
A reference collection that supports research into the geography, climate, government, and people of the different countries.
A list of topics to be included in research report.
Project booklet covers or folders.

Procedures
1. Introduce the concept of setting and its impact on story.
2. Give each student a map. (Or keep maps in a notebook which is held by the library media or classroom teacher.)
3. Have students select a story that has an identifiable foreign country setting.
4. Students read the story and schedule an oral book report with either the library media or classroom teacher.
5. When the report is made, the student colors in the country represented on the map, and does the follow-up research report.
6. The completed research reports are filed in the notebook next to the student's map. (A set of folders may be used instead of a notebook.)

Student Products
A booklet or folder including the world map and research reports made on the various countries.

Time Commitment
One class period to launch the project.
A year long reading project with the expectation of two books being read per month. The project could be shortened to a semester or marking period depending on the size of the collection, interest of students, or other demands in the classroom.

Adaptations
Biographies could be read in place of fiction using the country of the biographee for the follow-up research. Books set in different states could be used and the project could be limited to the U.S.A.

Sample Worksheet

READ YOUR WAY AROUND THE WORLD

1. You will deliver to the total class the monthly book report which is assigned by your classroom teacher. (Written report)

2. You will work with a teacher and independently on additional book reports.

   A) Complete a minimum of two books during the month.

   B) Books are to be selected based upon their settings—a foreign country.

   C) You will be given a world map. You will color in the country (on the map) showing where your book was set.

   D) You will schedule with your classroom or library media teacher a time to give an oral book report. (This will involve sitting down together and talking about the book.)

   E) The library media teacher will keep a card file of titles of books you read.

   F) Upon completing the book you will do some research on the country.

   The finished project of this research will be a paper consisting of one paragraph on each of the following topics and a bibliography.

      I. Geography
     II. Climate
    III. People
    IV. Government

   G) You will compile a booklet containing the research information about the countries you have read about.

The whole waiting   world is for you!

Story-grams

Concepts

Stories have similar identifiable elements.

Materials

Ditto of the story-gram or puzzle sheet for each student.
Copy of one story to serve as common experience.
Transparency of the story-gram.
Collection of short narratives; e.g., basal reader, collection of folk tales, short stories or novels suitable for book reports.

Procedures

1. Using transparency of story-gram (see sample with illustrations), discuss each of the elements in sequence, making certain that students can recognize examples of each element from stories already read. For example, identifying Wilbur's goal in *Charlotte's Web* as "staying alive," or hiding Miss Osborne, the mop, from adults in the household as the problem faced by the characters in the book of the same name.
2. Read a very simple (picture book) story to the class.
3. Have students identify the story elements while the teacher fills in the transparency as a model for students to view.
4. Give each student a ditto sheet of the story-gram. (See sample without illustrations.)
5. Assign a reading selection for the student to read and analyze.

Student Products

Filled-in ditto sheet of the story-gram.

Time Commitment

One class period for presentation.
Appropriate time for reading, depending upon length of assigned stories.
Filling in of story-gram is done concurrently with reading of the story.

Adaptations

Use story-gram information to develop a written book report.
Use information written on story-gram to compare and contrast folk tales from different countries.
Provide a filled-in story-gram for the student to use as a basis for creative writing activity.
Let the student fill in a story-gram and write a story based on this story-gram.

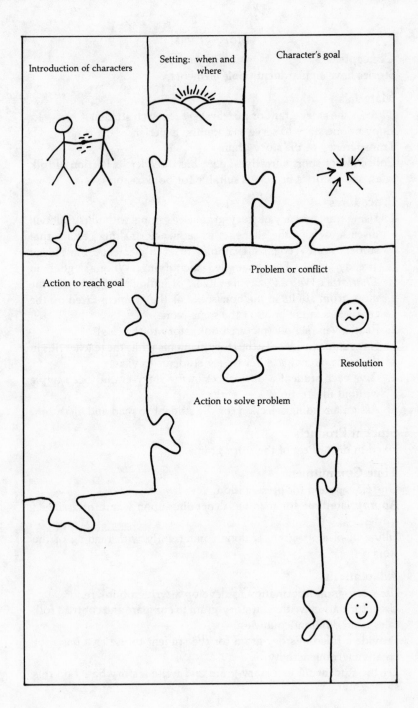

Introduction of characters

Setting: when and where

Character's goal

Action to reach goal

Problem or conflict

Action to solve problem

Resolution

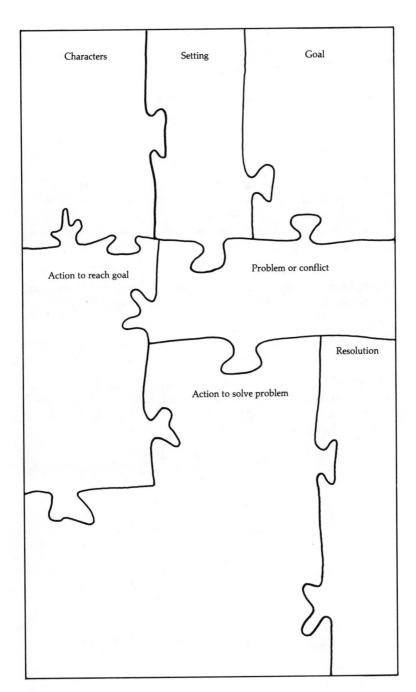

Characters

Setting

Goal

Action to reach goal

Problem or conflict

Resolution

Action to solve problem

Follow-up activity for an individual fiction title

Concepts
Critical reading skills which vary with the story.

Materials
Selected titles of fiction.
Worksheets designed to match those titles.

Procedures
1. Select a book and read it.
2. Develop activities related to the content of the story.
3. Activities should require creative thinking, not be limited to simple recall of facts. (See samples.)
4. Have student select a book to read and complete the accompanying worksheet.

Student Products
Completed worksheet activities. (Maps, pictures, poems, glossary of terms, or bibliography, etc.)

Time Commitment
Varies according to difficulty of book and accompanying activities. Probably two to three weeks.

Adaptations
Keep expanding the collection for which worksheets are developed. Students might read additional titles and suggest appropriate activities to be used on worksheets.

Sample Worksheet #1

FOLLOW-UP ACTIVITIES FOR: *The Mural Master* by Jones

1. Make a glossary of people, places, and things mentioned in the book. (Minimum of fifteen entries in your glossary.)
2. Use this chart format and fill in the needed information:

CHARACTER	LINE FROM THE PROPHESY	TASK

3. Draw a map of this fantasy land. Show where each group lives, the governmental headquarters, and as many specific places as you can.
4. Do A or B.
   A. Whose task was the hardest and why?
   B. Whose task was the easiest and why?
5. Prepare a bibliography on Wales using the library media center collection.

or

6. Find out as much as you can about the Welsh language—its pronunciation rules in particular.

Sample Worksheet #2

FOLLOW-UP ACTIVITIES FOR: *Blue Fin* by Thiele

Define these twelve words which are used in the book.

1. chumming
2. squids
3. continental shelf
4. riptide
5. plimsoll
6. pernickity
7. ludicrous
8. malicious
9. mollified
10. stentorian
11. obsequiously
12. inscrutable

Activities to do: Choose any four.

1. Choose one scene with detailed description. Draw a picture or make a diorama of it.
2. Research the author's background. Write up your findings.
3. Make a time-line of the major events of the book.
4. Make a chart listing Snook's strengths and weaknesses.
5. Judging by the repairs made on the Dog Star, what do you think might have caused it to be lost at sea?
6. Make a family tree for Snook's family. For each person make a list of words you could use to describe them.
7. Plot the steps involved from the preparation for the tuna fishing voyage to the finished can of tuna. Be as complete as possible.
8. Do the events after the water spout seem reasonable to you? Why or why not? Support your opinions with facts from the story.

Further Research:

1. Make as complete a bibliography as you can for "Australia" using the library media center collection.

or

2. Make a complete bibliography for the subject "Fish" using the library media center collection.

Sample Worksheet #3

FOLLOW-UP ACTIVITIES FOR: *The Gammage Cup* by Kendall

1. Refer to the list on page 26. What do each of the abbreviations really stand for?
2. Using the format of this chart fill in the information:

OUTLAWED CHARACTER	COLOR CHOICE	PERSONALITY TRAITS

3. Which of the characters do you most respect or admire? Why? Use details from the story to support your opinion.
4. A. Create your own additions to Gummy's Scribbles. (Minimum of eight lines of poetry.)
   or
   B . Create your own additions to Muggle's Maxims. (Minimum of four.)
5. Prepare a bibliography of "Gold Mining" using the library media center collection.
   or
6. Research armor and briefly describe the various types. Make a diagram of European armor of the 15th or 16th century labeling the parts.

Two of a kind

Concepts
Similarity of theme when characters and settings are different.

Materials
Pairs of books in which thematic similarities can be identified. For example, *Shelter from the Wind* by Bauer and *The Loner* by Wier (generation gap and runaways), *Incident At* or *Hawk Hill* by Eckert and *Bushbabies* by Stevenson (interdependence of people and animals for survival).

Procedures
1. Initial discussion of a theme element in stories.
2. Construct a chart which categorizes books by theme with titles drawn from students' previous reading experiences.
3. Emphasize that within stories that exemplify a given theme, there are similarities and differences.
4. Assign a pair of books which share a theme to each student. (This can be done by having titles and authors typed on a 3x5 card and have the student draw a card from the pack.)
5. Direct the students to read both books and make a list of similarities and differences in the stories.

Student Products
A written list of similarities and differences within the stories read, or an essay developed from this list.

Time Commitment
One class period for discussion.
Appropriate time for reading the stories; probably two to four weeks.

Adaptations
Paired selections could be biographical rather than fictional.

Role of fact and fantasy within a book

Concepts
Stories combine elements of fact and fantasy.

Materials
A collection of stories that are good examples of combined fact and fantasy such as *Miss Osborne the Mop* by Gage; *Black and Blue Magic* by Snyder; *Genie of Sutton Place* by Selden; *The Borrowers* by Norton; *Loretta Mason Potts* by Chase; *Twenty-one Balloons* by Du Bois; *Trumpet of the Swan* by White; or *The Lion, the Witch, and the Wardrobe* by Lewis.

Procedures
1. Assemble collection of stories to be read.
2. Hold discussion with students which enables them to identify fact and fantasy.
3. Assign or allow students to select a story from the collection.
4. Have students read the stories looking for elements of fact and fantasy within those stories.
5. Students share their reading experiences by presenting their lists of fact and fantasy orally.

Student Products
Student makes a list of elements of the story which are fact and another which are fantasy.

Student determines whether the story is more in the category of fact or fantasy.

Time Commitment
One class period for presentation.

Appropriate time for reading depending upon length of assigned stories; probably one or two weeks.

One class session to share reactions.

Adaptations
Move over to journalism and look for fact and opinion in newspaper and magazine articles.

Open-ended Activities

Open-ended activities are structured to provide outlets for creativity, originality, and divergent thinking. They rely heavily on verbal skills and call for unique interpretations.

Questioning skill development #1
Analyzing Questions Asked

Concepts
1. Asking questions is a means of gaining information.
2. Some questions are more helpful than others in terms of the amount of information they gain.
3. Listening to other people's questions can give you information too.

Materials
A list of objects to be guessed by students.

Procedures
1. Make a list of objects which could be used for a game of twenty questions.
2. Explain to the students that they may take turns asking questions which can be answered with yes or no.
3. Begin the game.
4. As questions are asked have students analyze their usefulness in reaching the final answer.
5. Point out that to begin with questions which help categorize or limit the field are more helpful than questions about specifics. For example, if the game began, "I am thinking of something and it is an animal," questions such as, "Is it a mammal?" or "Is it a reptile?" would be more helpful than asking, "Is it a dog?" or "Is it a snake?"
6. Play a number of rounds having students analyze their questioning strategy.

Student Products
Verbal participation during the game.

Time Commitment
One class period, repeated as desired.

Adaptations

Have students think of the next object. The student who guessed the last one correctly may have the right to a turn or students can take turns in order to allow everyone a chance.

Students could be put in teams. See which team can arrive at the solution in the shortest time or with the fewer questions. Groups would need to be positioned so as not to hear each other's questions. They would need to work quietly.

Questioning skill development #2
Asking questions to solve a problem

Concepts
1. Asking questions is a means of gaining information.
2. Questions related to the overall structure of the problem are more helpful than questions raised to a specific segment of the problem.
3. Questions can be categorized according to characteristics of the question itself. For example, some questions request information, some show evidence of drawing a conclusion based upon known facts, some are out and out guesses, while others ignore previous information or feedback from earlier questions.

Materials
Problem grids reproduced on a transparency or a ditto.

Procedures
1. Construct grids to be used. (see samples)
2. Develop symbol system based upon a set of rules. (see samples)
3. Give students the following directions:
   Each puzzle is made up of a pattern using a set of rules which are consistently applied in that puzzle. Your job is to discover the rules and to recreate the symbol pattern on the grid by asking questions. For each puzzle you will try to figure out what symbols are used and where they go.
   Ask any kind of questions whatever, including what symbol goes in a specific section if you wish. Ask questions which will give you information to help solve the puzzles.
   To help you ask questions, letters or numbers have been printed in the puzzle sections. These have absolutely nothing to do with the solution. They are there to help you and the teacher communicate when asking and answering questions. You may write on your puzzle grid if you wish.
4. Work with students individually or in groups. A group format allows students to build upon each other's work.
5. When students think they have solved the problem, let them try to fill in the remaining grid sections.
6. Verify their solution. Have student tell the rules being applied.

Student Products
Completed puzzle grids.

Time Commitment
One class period, repeated as desired.

Adaptations
Have students develop additional grids and symbol systems to swap with each other. As students gain experience the puzzles can become more and more complicated.

Practice Problem

System: 3 sided sections call for a ☆
          4 sided sections call for a ☽

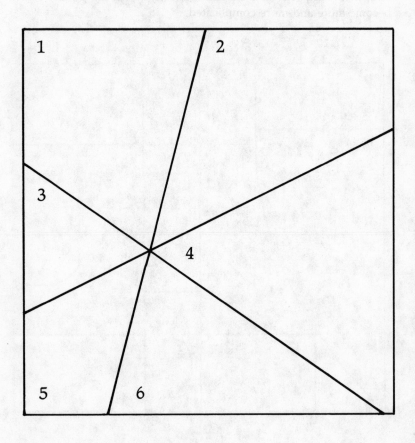

Sample Problem 1

System: space with base greater than height is identified with an X;
space with curved border is identified with a Y;
all other areas are identified with a Z.

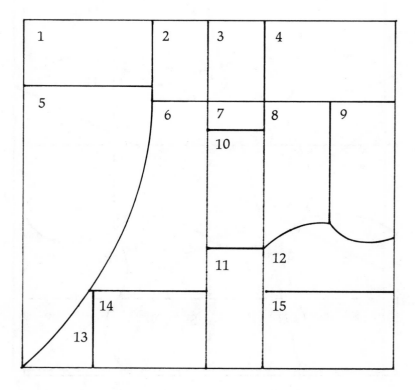

Sample Problem 2

System: Solid border equals A;
              Dotted border equals B;
              Number indicate how many of each; i.e.,
              section Q is 2A 2B and section R is 1A 3B.

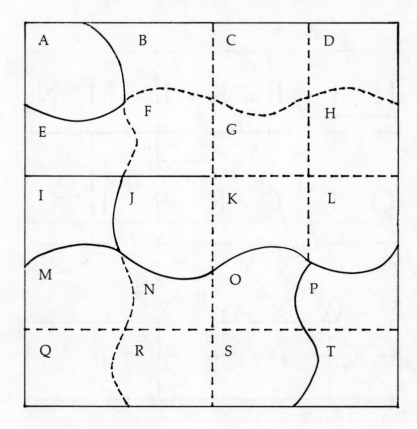

A   B   C   D   E   F   G

— — — — — — —

H   I   J   K   L   M   N

— — — — — — —

O   P   Q   R   S   T   U

— — — — — — —

V   W   X   Y   Z

— — — — —

System: Letters constructed with all straight lines are 1's;
with curved lines are 2's;
with a combination of curved and straight lines are 3's;
i.e., N is a 1, O is a 2, and P is a 3.

Sample Problem 4

System: Crossing a dotted line adds 5;
Crossing a solid line subtracts 3;
Crossing a curved line multiplies by 2.
The number 4 is assigned as a starting point in A,
progressing to P (488) as follows:

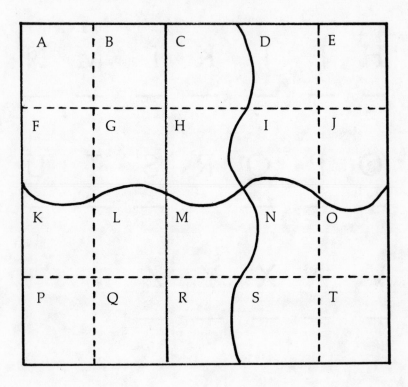

English word-roots, prefixes, and suffixes

Concepts
1. Long words are a succession of components with identifiable meanings of their own.
2. These component parts may be classified as prefixes, suffixes, or roots.
3. Learning the meanings of these components makes it possible to extract meaning from an unfamiliar word.

Materials
Dictionary of English word-roots such as the lists of Greek and Latin stems and prefixes in the *Lincoln Library* or *Dictionary of English Word-Roots* by Robert W. L. Smith.
A list of selected word components.
A list of words to analyze which contain the selected word components.

Procedures
1. Using examples the students would be familiar with such as un- or non-, bi- or tri-, have students analyze unfamiliar words which make use of these same components.
2. Discuss with the students the value of being able to analyze unfamiliar words in terms of familiar components.
3. Hand out worksheet which requires the students to define component parts of words and to analyze unfamiliar words in terms of them.

Student Products
Completed worksheet.

Time Commitment
A single class session for introduction, and probably a week for completing the activity.

Adaptations
Using standard components as building blocks construct "new words." Look these up in an unabridged dictionary to see if a similar term exists.

Sample

WORD COMPONENTS WORKSHEET

Name _____

I. Below is a list of word components and their meanings—sort of a mini-dictionary—to use with the words found at the bottom of the page in Part II.

ate = that which	ized = made to be
auto = self	ling = little
bio = life	mal = bad
cide = to kill	my = state of being
col = to filter	od = smell
con = together	ology = study of
contra = opposite	ous = having the quality of
dict = to speak	per = through
ecto = out	potam = river
ette = small	pro = forward or before
gen = kind	sib = relative
hepat = liver	sui = self
hipp = horse	trans = across
homo = same	tympan = drum
itis = inflamation of	us = a Latin term ending

II. Divide the following words into their components.
Write individual components and their meanings.
Write the complete word and a dictionary type definition for it.
(Use meanings of components to build the definition of the total word).

Example: sui = self   cide = to kill
          suicide means to kill one's self

WORDS:

contradict	homogenized	sibling
hepatitis	malodorous	tympanectomy
hippopotamus	percolate	

98

Eponyms: People in words

Concepts
The name of the person who is involved with inventing, developing or marketing an item, often becomes part of the name of the item.

Materials
Selected list of eponyms.
An eponym dictionary.
Biographical references.

Procedures
1. Select eponyms to be used.
2. Verify that these individuals are included in the biographical references within the collection.
3. Explain the concept of eponyms.
4. Provide some examples.
5. Hand out worksheet and have students proceed. (See sample).

Student Products
Completed worksheet.

Time Commitment
One class session to introduce project and about a week to complete the project.

Adaptations
Have students bring in additional samples of eponyms to share with class.

Sample

EPONYM WORKSHEET

Name _____

For each of the following words, identify the person's name who is associated with it, and give the reason why. Consult dictionaries and biographical references to find your information.

Chauvinism

Boycott

Pants

Atlas

Silhouette

Cereal

Volcano

Sandwich

Poinsettia

Tangerine

Saxophone

Ammonia

Guillotine

Pasteurize

Titanic

Macadam

Turquoise

Limousine

Spaniel

Homonyms and humor

Concepts

1. Homonyms are words that sound alike when said but are spelled differently and have different meanings.
2. Humor is derived from the juxtaposition of meanings and spellings; e.g., calling a row of rabbits that disappear into the distance a receding (hair) hare line.

Materials

Dictionaries of homonyms.
Samples of humor derived from homonyms such as those in the book *Pun Fun* by Ennis Rees.

Procedures

1. Discuss homonyms with the students.
2. Have students give examples.
3. Introduce the element of humor by sharing examples and explaining them if necessary.
4. Identify possible sources for homonyms.
5. Ask students to select pairs of homonyms to use to create humorous statements.

Student Products

Humorous statements.

Time Commitment

Introduced in one class period.
One week of follow-up and more if interest warrants it.

Adaptations

Collect samples of humor based on homonyms such as cartoons, riddles, jokes and post these on a bulletin board.

Visual puns

Concepts
1. Awareness of multiple meanings of the same word.
2. Awareness of homonyms.
3. Awareness of puns as a type of humor.
4. Puns may be visual as well as verbal.

Materials
Sources of samples such as *Punography* books by *Bruce McMillan*, various pages in *Games Magazine*, or daily features such as those in the *Akron* (Ohio) *Beacon Journal*.
Materials required to produce student examples; i.e., video tape, photographic film for either slides or prints, or cut and paste or drawn pictures.

Procedures
1. Share some of the examples with participating students.
2. Discuss the nature of the humor used.
3. Have students suggest additional phrases which could be illustrated visually.
4. Determine medium to be used, and produce necessary artwork.
5. Share finished product with audience.

Student Products
Depending on the medium used, the finished products would be a set of posters, photographic slides or prints, video tape, etc.

Time Commitment
Somewhat dependent upon the medium used. Could be as short as a week or extend through a marking period.

Adaptations
Terms could be limited to a particular field such as sports, history, science.
Common phrases could be used.
Could be a potential theme for a film festival.

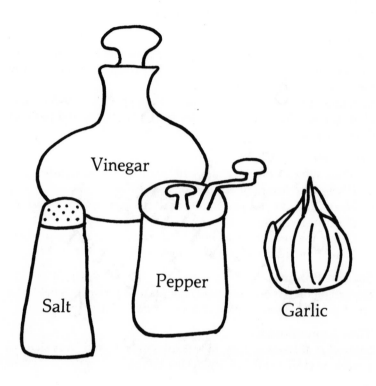

(The Four Seasons)

wether

WHETHER

weater

(a bad spell of weather)

Signs—symbols, icons, and symbolic icons

Concepts

1. Signs are used to communicate.
2. Signs may be symbols, icons, and/or symbolic icons.
3. A symbol only has meaning when people agree upon that meaning. Examples: written language, musical notation, map symbols.
4. An icon derives its meaning from resemblance to the actual object. For example, models, photographs, miniatures, etc.
5. Messages can be misunderstood when an icon is used as a symbol (symbolic icon). For example, the sun at the horizon may be sunrise or sunset; the use of the White House, in addition to being the White House, can mean The Presidency, Washington, D.C., government, etc.
6. Semiotics is the term used for the study of signs.

Materials

A collection of pictures clipped from magazines.
A collection of photographs, charts, musical scores, maps, etc.
Books showing signs and symbols and their meanings.

Procedures

1. Initiate a discussion with the phrase "A picture is worth a thousand words."
2. Examine the idea that a thousand pictures could also be needed to fully explain a single word. Examples could be a picture of an elephant which saves many words while it would take many pictures to explain fully the meaning of the word 'mammal'.
3. Examine sample pictures which illustrate the activity's concepts.
4. Classify pictures as symbols, icons, and/or symbolic icons.

Student Products

A set of pictures grouped according to categories discussed.

Time Commitment

One class period.

Adaptations

Look for signs that are not man-made, such as weather (2" rain in a bucket that was empty before the storm), gardening (leaves on house plant turn yellow from lack of light, or cracked ground indicating lack of rain), or disasters (smoke pouring from a window in your house).
Look for examples of body language such as smiles, frowns, positioning of hands.

Observing details

Concepts
1. There is a difference between observing and seeing.
2. Observation skills can be improved through practice.

Materials
A set of items with common characteristics as well as with individual differences; e.g., a collection of shoes, seashells, animals, fabric swatches, etc.

Procedures
1. Discuss the differences between observing and seeing.
2. Have students select a specific object from the collection provided.
3. Have student write a brief description of the item highlighting differences unique to the item.
4. Share the descriptions verbally having other members of the group try to identify the specific item. (If written work is read by the teacher the students can not identify the item by knowing who wrote about it).
5. Discuss the strengths and weaknesses of the descriptions.

Student Products
Written descriptions and participation in verbal identifications.

Time Commitment
A single class period.

Adaptations
Describe non-visual characteristics such as personality traits or emotions.

Sample

DESCRIPTIONS OF ANIMALS

This animal is 15 inches long. Her tail is 12 inches long and very bushy. Her fur is very soft and long. The color is black, and a white stripe runs down her back and tail. (Skunk)

This animal is 5 inches long with a 2 inch tail. The fur is very short. Most of the animal is rust colored, but there are dark and light stripes down the back. (Chipmunk)

This animal has very, very soft fur. It is dark brown. Its tail is long and thin with no fur on it. Its feet are webbed and its ears do not stick out. (Muskrat)

Creating mental images from printed passages

Concepts

1. A mental image reflects one's level of comprehension.
2. Reading is more pleasurable when one produces mental images from the content being read.
3. Mental images improve with practice; i.e., they become more detailed, more accurate, more automatic.
4. There is a relationship between an individual's skill in producing mental images and the breadth of his/her background knowledge.

Materials

Written passages to be read selected for their potential for generating mental images.

Procedures

1. Read a passage and ask students what they "see."
2. Elaborate on student responses, showing the potential of the passage by pointing out what was overlooked.
3. Continue with additional examples.

Student Products

Contributions to the discussions.

Time Commitment

One class period repeated at various times.

Adaptations

Have students write passages for other students to visualize.

When examining several passages selected from the works of authors exhibiting distinctive styles, be able to group passages according to author.

Examples might include the works of:

> Joel Chandler Harris
> Dr. Seuss
> Charles Dickens
> Bret Harte
> Agatha Christie

Synthesis activity

Concepts
1. By examining a cluster of specifics, one can arrive at a generalization.
2. To evaluate the correctness of this generalization, verify that each specific has been considered.

Materials
Appropriate reference collection.
Sets of clues; i.e., specifics related to an item.

Procedures
1. Think of items for which suitable clues could be developed.
2. Select a format for distributing clues; e.g., worksheet, bulletin board, learning center, etc.
3. Produce appropriate clue sets. (If the item is a place, clues should be related to geography, climate, events, products, holidays and celebrations. If it is an animal, clues relate to physical description, habitat, food, shelter, life cycle, geographic distribution, etc.)
4. Develop a set of directions and explain them to students.
5. Distribute clue sets and let students begin work.

Student Products
A written list of items indicated by the clues.

Time Commitment
Could be a series used once a week as an enrichment activity, or a group of activities combined on one worksheet.
In the latter case, one or two weeks should suffice.

Adaptations
Difficulty of clues can be adjusted to the skill level of the group.

SYNTHESIS ACTIVITY WORKSHEET

Name _____

Directions:
Identify the person, place or thing that is described by the set of clues. Make certain that your answer incorporates *all* clues.

Set 1.
Lasted from 1775 to 1783.
Began with the battles of Lexington and Concord.
The winter at Valley Forge was a low point.
Ended with the signing of the Treaty of Paris.
The enemy wore red coats.
Resulted in formation of U.S.A.
Is also called War of American Independence.

Answer _____

Set 2.
Has six petals.
Blossoms are purple, yellow, or white.
Arching, grass-like foliage.
Blooms in early spring.
Grows best where there are cold winters.
Foliage withers when mature and
makes plant invisible in summer.   Answer _____

Set 3.
Is located on the River Seine.
Residents speak French.
Home of the Eiffel Tower.
The Mona Lisa hangs in the Louvre.
Bastille Day parades march down the Champs Elysees.
Famous for sidewalk cafes.
Lindbergh landed at this city.   Answer _____

Relative terms

Concepts
1. Familial relationships are identified by specific terms such as grandparents, cousins, in-laws, etc.
2. Some terms indicate blood relationships while others indicate relationships by marriage.

Materials
A list of terms.

A number of narrative paragraphs which identify relationship among people that students will answer questions about. (See sample).

A list of questions which are applied to these paragraphs.

Procedures
1. Hand out list of terms.
2. Discuss meaning of terms with students.
3. Have students give examples from their own families; e.g., "I have six cousins, two aunts, and a grandmother living."
4. Identify the common ancestors for various relationships.
5. Discuss relationships in terms of age relationships; i.e., a parent or grandparent must be older than a child or grandchild, but this is not necessarily true of one's cousins, aunts, or uncles.
6. Classify relationships as being blood relations or related through marriage.
7. Hand out worksheets and verify students' understanding of relationships by having students answer the questions. The narrative paragraphs supply the necessary facts.

Student Products
Completed worksheet.

Time Commitment
One class period with follow-up as necessary.

Adaptations
Each student could prepare a family tree. This tree could be either factual or fictional.

Sample Questions

RELATIVE TERMS WORKSHEET

What term or terms could be used to describe the relationship of this person to you:

1. Your mother's sister's child (first cousin)
2. Your grandmother's daughter's husband (father or uncle)
3. Your father's first cousin's child? (second cousin)

Who would the parents of your stepbrother be? (the husband or wife of mother or father and someone else)

Who would the parents of your half sister be? (mother or father and someone else)

List three terms which are associated with blood relationships. (brother, sister, grandmother)

List three terms which are associated with relationship by marriage. (sister-in-law, stepfather, mother-in-law)

You and your first cousin share which ancestors? (grandparents)

Creating idioms

Concepts

1. An idiom is an expression whose meaning can not be derived from its component parts.
2. Idioms are not translatable directly from one language to another.

Materials

Dictionary of idioms, or a list of idioms.

A worksheet listing idioms to be defined by students, along with space to create originals.

Procedures

1. Develop a list of idioms to be used on the worksheet.
2. Create the worksheet. (See sample.)
3. Discuss idioms as an aspect of language. Share examples.
4. Hand out worksheet and have students begin.

Student Products

Completed worksheet including at least one original "idiom" with its definition.

Time Commitment

One class period for presentation of concepts and a week to complete the activity.

Adaptations

Collect idioms from different languages and look for similarities of thought.

Sample

IDIOMATIC EXPRESSIONS

Name _____

I. For each of the following idiomatic expressions, give

   A. the idiomatic meaning of the phrase, and

   B. an explanation of the relationship between the idiomatic and literal meanings.

1. _____

   A. _____

   B. _____

2. _____

   A. _____

   B. _____

ETC.

II. Create an original idiom and give its meaning.

_____

_____

SAMPLE IDIOMS:

It's a lemon.

Has the cat got your tongue?

What a can of worms!

Don't take any wooden nickles.

Create a private code

Concepts

1. A code is a system of symbols used for brevity or secrecy of communication.
2. Rules that can be consistently applied must be developed to produce a code.

Materials

Books on codes and ciphers.

Procedures

1. Discuss the use of codes throughout history.
2. Use some specific code systems as examples; e.g., Morse Code, wartime codes.
3. Discuss types of codes in terms of complexity.
4. Challenge students to create their own codes.

Student Products

A written set of rules for applying the code devised.
A sample message written in the code.

Time Commitment

Open-ended.

Adaptations

Challenge each other to crack coded messages.

Sample Codes

1. In Morse Code, a system of combining dots, dashes, and spaces to represent letters, numbers, etc., the name 'Tim Smith' would look like this: —   ..   — —

      ...   — —   ..   —   ....

2. A common device is to assign a number to each letter of the alphabet and write the message using the numbers for the letters. Such a code would look like this:

Come at six o'clock.   3 15 13 5   1 20   19 9 24   15 3 12 15 3 11.

3. In some cases a copy of the key is needed to interpret the code. For example, when the alphabet is simply staggered, it is used twice with the second line being the letters used to write the message. It would look like this:

                                  (Normal use)

A B C D E F G H I J K L M N O P Q R S T U V W X Y Z
d e f g h i j k l m n o p q r s t u v w x y z a b c

                                  (Coded use)

Come at six o'clock.   Frph dw vla rforfn.

4. Some codes are designed to use a matrix such as the following:

ABC	DEF	GHI
JKL	MNO	PQR
STU	VWX	YZ

Come at six o'clock.

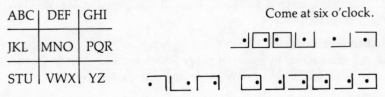

Selected Titles of Books on Codes and Ciphers:
Norman, Bruce. *Secret Warfare*. Acropolis Books, 1973.
Peck, Lyman C. *Secret Codes, Remainder Arithmetic and Matrices*. National Council of Teachers of Mathematics, 1961.
Sinkov, Abraham. *Elementary Cryptanalysis*. Random House, 1968.
Way, Peter. *Codes and Ciphers*. Crescent Books, 1976.

Design a game

Concepts

1. When designing a game, there is need to balance the effects of skill and luck on the playing of the game.
2. Categories of games; e.g., board, card, tile, or lotto types.
3. The importance of planning; i.e., a mock-up or draft to use in testing playability.

Materials

Whatever supplies are required for producing the game parts, as well as reference materials to support the research component.

Procedures

1. Let the students play games of various types and formats. Discuss what they like about favorite games, and what they do not like about others.
2. Discuss the roles of luck and skill in each of the games.
3. Assign the students the task of designing and developing a game related to a unit of study.
4. Have the students research the chosen subject matter and decide upon a format for their game.
5. Have the students make a mock-up or rough draft of the game.
6. Have the students write out a set of directions.
7. Before the students make a finished set of game pieces, have small groups of students test-play the games. Once the complications are worked out, have the students make the final product.

Student Products

A game related to a unit of study which includes a set of instructions and all the necessary pieces for playing the game.

Time Commitment

A month to a marking period depending upon the amount of time devoted to the project.

Adaptations

Have students design games for use with younger students as a service to the school.

Have students make adaptations to existing commercial games in order to increase their teaching value.

Interdisciplinary Activities

Higher level thinking skills such as analysis, synthesis, and evaluation are required in interdisciplinary activities. Skills and background information which may seem unrelated are re-examined and restructured. Activities of this sort serve to reduce students' tendencies to view information in isolation, and encourage recognition of relationships.

Webbing as a means of visualizing relationships

Concepts
1. Webbing visualizes organizational structure of content.
2. Webbing shows multiple interrelationships.
3. Webbing can be free flowing or rigidly structured.

Materials
Sample web layouts done on transparencies.
Content to be webbed, possibly a story to be read aloud to group, known mathematical facts, basic concepts such as size, color, or shape of familiar objects.

Procedures
1. Select an appropriate layout to match the material to be webbed.
2. Identify the content to be webbed. This would mean reading a story aloud, discussing such concepts as color, size, shape.
3. Have the group make contributions and record them.

Student Products
These will vary according to the specifics of the lesson. Sometimes an individual web will be produced; in other cases, information on the group-produced web might be used as the basis for a picture, a paragraph, poem, etc. (See samples.)

Time Commitment
One class session for explanations.
Not more than a week for individual work.

Adaptations
Webs can be designed for drill as in math facts, for alternative book report formats, and as an alternative to traditional outlining.

Sample Follow up Activity

WEB FOR ANDY'S SQUARE BLUE ANIMAL

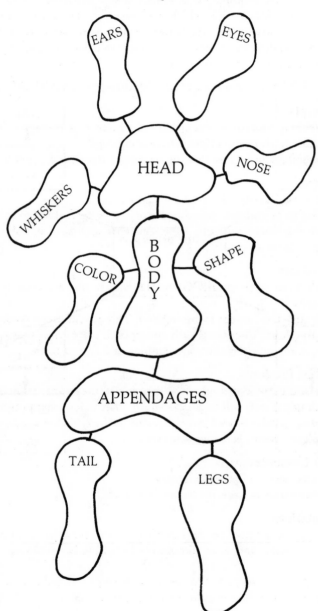

Sample

Biography Web Format

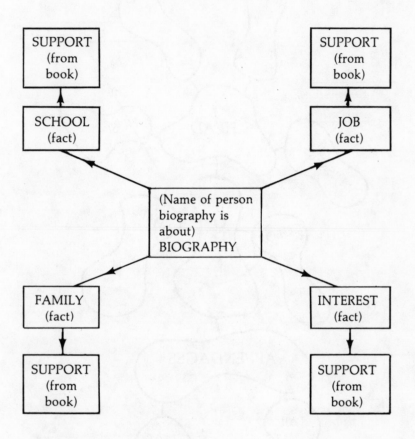

Information in CAPITALS is on the web when handed out.
Information in parentheses is what student fills in.

Sample

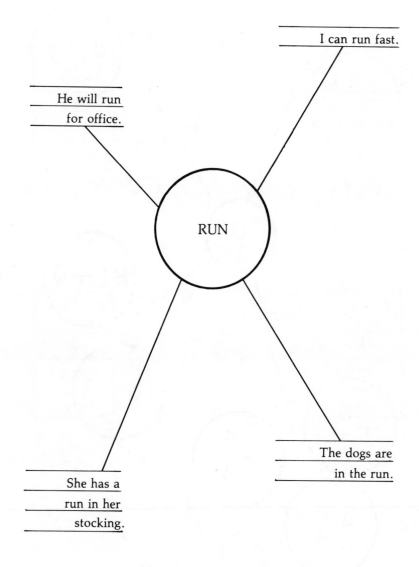

I can run fast.

He will run
for office.

RUN

She has a
run in her
stocking.

The dogs are
in the run.

Sample

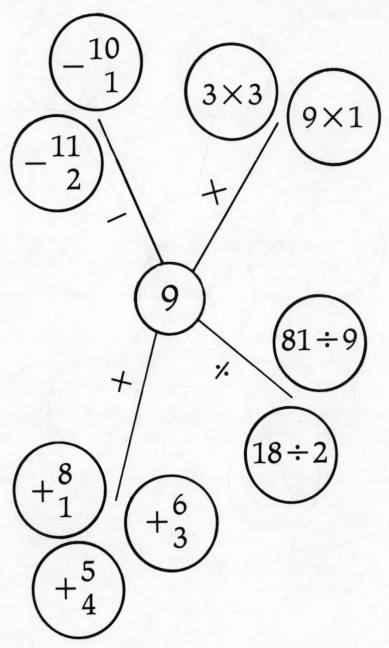

Sample

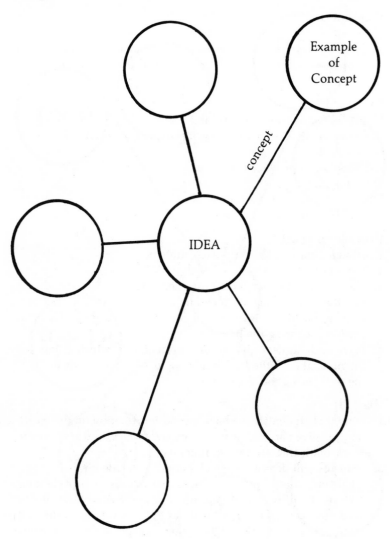

National park project

Concepts
1. Need for pre-planning of a trip.
2. Need to base decisions on such things as time, distance, and economic factors in travel, and personal preferences, interests, and priorities.

Materials
Visitor's guides, travel guides, and maps.
Reference materials such as encyclopedias and specialized regional books.
Art supplies to produce brochures.
Ditto for itinerary.
Outline map to plot the route.
Assignment hand out.

Procedures (Part I)
1. Assign a national park to each student.
2. On a large wall map locate each park.
3. Have students research their assigned park in order to produce a brochure describing its location and size, scenic attractions, history, facilities. Have them include a bibliography of sources used in preparing the brochure.
4. Have each student give an oral presentation which points out the highlights of the park studied and which attempts to "sell" the park as a good vacation place.

(Part II)
1. Now that students have background information on the parks, they are given an outline map, a calendar page, and are asked to block out a three-week trip itinerary.
2. Students will determine which parks to include on their "trip."
3. Guidelines should point out potential pitfalls in trip planning such as the difficulty of getting from point A to point B, the need to consider such realities of travel as time for transportation, meals, sight-seeing, sleep, and the expense involved for each of these.
4. The completed trip will be evaluated in terms of feasibility.

Student Products
A brochure on an individual park.
An outline map with a trip drawn in.
An itinerary page to match the trip planned.

Time Commitment
At least a marking period.

Adaptations
Compute cost factor of the trip as planned.

Sample

NATIONAL PARK PROJECT

Part I. Design a brochure describing the National Park assigned to you. Include the following topics:

1. location and size
2. scenic attractions
3. history of park
4. facilities
5. bibliography

Part II. One large map will be made of the United States. Each park will be identified on this class map. Each student will report orally on the highlights of his or her brochure to the rest of the class.

Part III. Each student will be given an outline map on which to plot his or her individual trip. Each student will be given a blank calendar page to block out a three week itinerary. In planning the itinerary, thought must be given to the following concerns:

time for—
1. transportation
2. meals
3. sight-seeing
4. sleeping

and money for—
1. transportation
2. meals
3. lodging
4. sight-seeing
5. souvenirs

A variety of skills will be incorporated into this project including: language arts, math, science, geography, search skills, art, and map reading.

Decorate your room project

Concepts
1. Interpreting mail order catalogs.
2. Interior design concept of color, layout, traffic patterns, energy factors, style, function of room, etc.
3. Pros and cons of credit.

Materials
A variety of mail order catalogs such as Penny's, or Sears'.
Reference materials to provide basic rules for interior decoration.
Sample order forms.
Graph paper for scale layouts.
Box and art supplies for constructing diorama.
Assignment handout.

Procedures
1. Hand out the worksheet.
2. Help student learn how to identify relevant information from the catalog description of items.
3. Help student learn how to fill out an order form correctly.
4. Discuss effects of color, style, patterns and layout using pictures of sample rooms in books and magazines.
5. Have student make selections and actually fill out sample order form including tax and shipping costs.
6. Have student use box and various art supplies to make a diorama of the room as designed.
7. Have the student draw a floor plan to scale using dimensions and directions provided in the handout.

Student Products
Completed order form
A diorama.
A scale floor plan.

Time Commitment
About four weeks.

Adaptations
Redesign the classroom and use catalogs for school equipment.

Sample

DECORATE YOUR ROOM PROJECT

1. Using the catalogs provided, or any others you have at home, look for items you would like to use to decorate your bedroom. Pretend you are moving to a brand new house. All that is there is an empty shell of a room 9x12′. You need to decorate it (floor covering, wall covering, window treatment, etc.); furnish it (bed, desk, chest, chair, etc.); and personalize it (posters, hobby items, lamps, etc.).

2. Fill out the order blank. Read it carefully and be sure to put down all the information that is asked for. Accuracy is vital! Use the chart to figure tax and postage charges. Add correctly.

3. Use a shoe box or container of similar size and make a mock-up of the room you design. You can draw the items and paste them in place or make them three dimensional.

4. Draw a floor plan to scale. Make one-half inch equal one foot of actual space. Make the furniture the same scale and place it the way you want it to be in the real room. Sample below.

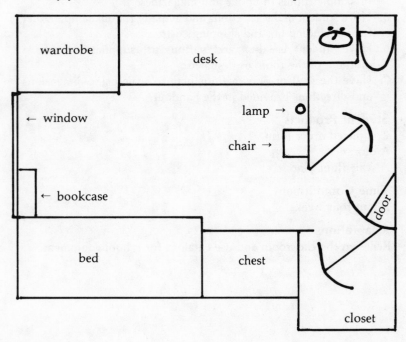

Index of Activities
Arranged by Time Commitment

Activities requiring a single class period

Analyzing questions asked
Asking questions to solve a problem
Atlas activity for Hallowe'en
Bibliographic forms
Creating mental images from printed passages
Introduction to indexes
Observing details
Outlining activity
Relative terms
Signs—symbols, icons, symbolic icons
Two ways to alphabetize

Activities requiring one to two weeks of work time

Acronyms activity
Application of two ways to alphabetize
Atlas index activity
Biographical dictionary of fiction book characters
Contemporaries activity
Creating idioms
English word-roots, prefixes, and suffixes
Eponyms: people in words
Find the fact (index)
Finding a fact (general encyclopedia)
Follow-up activity for an individual fiction title
Homonyms and humor
Interpreting abbreviations used in indexes of
  multi-volumed works
Introduction to encyclopedias: finding an entry
Role of fact and fantasy within a book
Scavenger hunt (index)

Skimming for specific information #1
Skimming for specific information #2
Specialized dictionaries activity
Specialized reference books: overview
Story-grams
Synthesis activity
Table of contents activity: find the fact
Thematic find a specific fact (general encyclopedia)
Trace name across U.S.A. (atlas)
Two of a kind
Use of subheadings
Using indexes to create a bibliography
Webbing as a means of visualizing relationships

Activities requiring a month, a marking period, or longer
Around the year with poetry
Calendar of famous firsts and unusual events
Collect postmarks
Conducting a poll on a topic of concern
Create a hall of fame
Create a private code
Decorate your room
Design a game
National park project
Read your way around the world
School-wide postal system
Thematic report writing using a common outline
Visual puns

Appendix 1
Problem-Solving Materials

Problem-solving activities provide gifted and talented students with valuable learning experiences. Recent interest in programs for the gifted has led to the proliferation of commercially produced materials designed to teach problem-solving skills. Many of these materials do provide excellent learning experiences, emphasizing higher levels of thinking skills. Unfortunately other materials, while using the term problem-solving in their titles, emphasize low level rote/recall type activities. As is true when ordering materials related to any subject area, it is important to evaluate problem-solving materials carefully. The list which follows provides a sampling of materials which give practice in problem-solving skills. It is not intended to be an exhaustive list, but rather a place to begin.

1. Bereiter, Carl and Anderson, Valerie
Willy the Wisher and Other Thinking Stories
Open Court Pub. Co.   La Salle, Ill. 61301   1970

A collection of 50 stories designed to be read to youngsters. As the story unfolds, questions are inserted which ask the child to think ahead about the characters in the story. Characters have outstanding peculiarities in their thinking which youngsters learn to recognize and avoid in their own thinking.

2. Covington, Martin, Crutchfield, Richard, Davies, Lillian and Olton Jr, Robert
The Productive Thinking Program
Charles E. Merrill Pub. Co.
1300 Alum Creek Dr., Columbus, Ohio 43216   1974

By solving mysteries presented in a series of fifteen booklets, upper elementary grade students develop the following skills: 1) recognizing puzzling facts, 2) asking relevant questions, 3) generating ideas, 4) seeing problems in new ways, 5) evaluating ideas, and 6) solving problems.

131

3. Daniel, Becky and Charlie
Thinker Sheets
Good Apple, Inc.
Box 229, Carthage, Ill. 62321

Includes a series of activities designed to develop skills associated with following directions. Many activities do not have one correct answer, thus encouraging students to give a rationale for their answers. Good activities for primary grades. Activities can serve as patterns for students to create additional similar activities.

4. Harnadek, Anita
Think About It—Basic Thinking Skills
Midwest Pub. Co.
P.O. Box 129, Troy, Mich. 48099

Helps develop a common-sense approach to problem solving which can be applied in all areas of the curriculum. Greater emphasis is placed upon students being able to give a reason for their answers than their exact answer. Format allows teachers to include some of the materials whenever the class has a few minutes to spare.

5. Renzulli, Joseph
New Directions in Creativity: Mark A, B, 1, 2, and 3
Harper and Row Pub. Co.   New York   1976

Activities included are designed to broaden the way youngsters look at their world. Skills to be developed include: 1) fluency (generate possibilities), 2) flexibility (use different approaches), 3) originality (produce unusual responses), and 4) elaboration (expand ideas).
Volume A is most successful with kindergarten and first grades.
Volume B with second and third graders, and Volumes 1–3 with grades four through eight.

6. Rubin, Dorothy
The Teacher's Handbook for Reading/Thinking Exercises
Holt, Rinehart and Winston   New York   1980

Activities in this volume deal with word meanings, and reasoning with verbal concepts. The activities concentrate on higher levels of comprehension skills and is appropriate for intermediate grade students and above.

7. Standish, Bob
Sunflowering

Good Apple Inc.
Box 229   Carthage, Ill.   62321   1977

Activities included fall into four categories of teaching/learning strategies: 1) Imagery analogies which describe the external world in personal terms, 2) Object-to-object analogies which compare seemingly unlike objects, 3) Person-to-object analogies which call for the personification of something, and 4) Transforming strategies which call for making changes in conditions within a situation.

8.   Synectics Inc.
Making it Strange Vol. 1–4
Harper and Row Pub.   New York   1968

Activities are designed to initiate creative writing based upon divergent thinking. Students are asked to assign emotions to objects, give physical characteristics such as weight to coughs and sneezes, and other similarly open-ended tasks.

9.   Tan, Ellen, et al.
Bright Ideas—Complete Enrichment Units
Creative Teaching Press Inc.
Monterey Park, Calif.   91754

A collection of lessons and activities chosen as most interesting by students from a gifted resource room. Background information for the teacher and activities for students related to eleven topics are included.

10.   Williams, Frank
Classroom Ideas for Encouraging Thinking and Feeling
D.O.K. Publishers, Inc.
Buffalo, New York 14214   1970

The activities included call for processes of inquiry, discovery, and creative problem solving. Instead of presenting the student with facts, these activities pose problems and creative situations for the students to react to. Activities are related to a variety of subject content areas. Cognitive and affective processes are encouraged.

Appendix 2
Minimum Reference Collection Suggestion

General Encyclopedias selected according to individual preference.

World Book, Comptons, New Book of Knowledge, etc.

Specialized Encyclopedias

Social Studies
> *Lands and Peoples* 7 vols. Grolier 1972
> *Worldmark Encyclopedia of the Nations* 5 vols. John Wiley and Sons 1971
> *Worldmark Encyclopedia of the States* Harper and Row Pub. 1981

Science
> *Book of Popular Science* Grolier 1974
> *The Illustrated Encyclopedia of the Animal Kingdom* Grolier 1972

Dictionaries

Webster's Third New International Dictionary
Beginning and intermediate dictionaries of your choice

Specialized Dictionaries

Dictionary of Mythology Centennial Press 1970
Oxford Dictionary of Nursery Rhymes Clarendon Press 1952
Dictionary of Cliches Routledge and Kegan Paul Ltd. 1960
Acronyms, Initialisms, and Abbreviations Dictionary Gale Research 1976
A Practical Dictionary of Rhymes Crown Pub. 1960
Dictionary of Word and Phrase Origins Vol. 1–3 Harper and Row Pub. 1962, 1967, & 1971
Foreign Language dictionaries of your choice
> *Cassell's German Dictionary* Funk and Wagnalls
> *Cassell's French Dictionary* Macmillan Pub.

Cassell's Spanish Dictionary Funk and Wagnalls
More Words of Science Houghton Mifflin 1972
The Crescent Dictionary of Mathematics Macmillan Co. 1962
The Dinosaur Dictionary The Citadel Press 1972
Dictionary of Fictional Characters The Writer, Inc. 1974
Webster's Biographical Dictionary G. & C. Merriam Co. 1972
Webster's Geographical Dictionary G. & C. Merriam Co.
Include other specialized dictionaries as desired

Atlas

Goode's World Atlas Rand McNally and Co. 1960
Shepherd's Historical Atlas Barnes and Noble 1964
Atlas of World Wildlife Rand McNally and Co. 1973
A United States Atlas of your choice

Biographical References

Who's Who Bowker 1971
Current Biography Wilson Co. annual yearbook
Something About the Author Gale Research

Specific Titles

Famous First Facts Wilson and Co.
An Almanac of your choice
Roget's Thesaurus St. Martin's Press 1962
Granger's Index to Poetry Columbia University Press 1973
Bartlett's Familiar Quotations Little, Brown and Co. 1980
Who Was When Wilson and Co. 1976
Rules of the Game Bantam Books 1975
Index to Illustrations of the Natural World Shoe String Press 1979
Index to Illustrations of Living Things Shoe String Press 1981
Facts about Presidents Wilson Co. 1974
Encyclopedia of How it is Made A. & W. Publishers Inc. 1978
Joy of Cooking Bobbs Merrill Co. 1975
Oxford Companion to Music Oxford University Press 1970
Art Through the Ages Harcourt Brace Jovanovich
Colonial Craftsmen World Pub. Co. 1965
Colonial Living World Pub. Co. 1957
Flags Through the Ages and Across the World McGraw Hill 1975
Costumes and Styles E. P. Dutton and Co. 1956
Celebrations—The Complete Book of American Holidays Doubleday 1972

Categories of Books to Be Included According to Your Need

Field Guides for identification of such things as birds, shells, trees, rocks and minerals, flowers, etc.

National Geographic and Time-Life titles related to science and social studies units.

General survey type book on topics of interest in your population. For example: cats, dogs, stamps, rocks, sports, Indians, etc.

The titles included in this list are meant to serve as suggestions of the types of materials which should be included in a reference collection. Specific titles can be substituted as long as the central features remain. The titles offered here are not meant to limit the collection, but rather to provide a base for a broader reference library.

Index